Praise for *The Idiot Factor*:

"Larry's frank, brutal, tough, and sometimes even obnoxious! But you know something? He has a big heart and an even bigger gut for how we can avoid big mistakes."
—Neil Cavuto, Fox News

"His advice . . . is so blunt and so true that it might keep you sane until you retire."
—Bloomberg News

"Larry Winget takes a tough love approach to helping you improve your life with this book but you'll be glad you read it. He doesn't mince words yet his advice for making more of yourself is spot on."
—Mark Sanborn, bestselling author of *The Fred Factor* and *You Don't Need a Title to Be a Leader*

"A bald-headed, cowboy-booted combination of Will Rogers, Norman Vincent Peale and Vince Lombardi, Larry Winget is an American treasure."
—James Bradley, *New York Times* bestselling author of *Flags of Our Fathers* and *Flyboys*

Larry Winget is one of the country's leading business speakers and is a regular guest on Fox News. He is the bestselling author of *No Time for Tact*; *You're Broke Because You Want to Be*; *It's Called Work for a Reason!*; and *Shut Up, Stop Whining & Get a Life*. He lives in Paradise Valley, Arizona.

THE
IDIOT
FACTOR

The 10 Ways We Sabotage
Our Life, Money, and Business

(Previously published as
People Are Idiots and I Can Prove It!)

LARRY WINGET

GOTHAM
BOOKS

GOTHAM BOOKS
Published by Penguin Group (USA) Inc.
375 Hudson Street, New York, New York 10014, U.S.A.

Penguin Group (Canada), 90 Eglinton Avenue East, Suite 700, Toronto, Ontario M4P
2Y3, Canada (a division of Pearson Penguin Canada Inc.); Penguin Books Ltd, 80
Strand, London WC2R 0RL, England; Penguin Ireland, 25 St Stephen's Green, Dublin
2, Ireland (a division of Penguin Books Ltd); Penguin Group (Australia), 250 Camberwell Road, Camberwell, Victoria 3124, Australia (a division of Pearson Australia Group
Pty Ltd); Penguin Books India Pvt Ltd, 11 Community Centre, Panchsheel Park, New
Delhi–110 017, India; Penguin Group (NZ), 67 Apollo Drive, Rosedale, North Shore
0632, New Zealand (a division of Pearson New Zealand Ltd); Penguin Books (South
Africa) (Pty) Ltd, 24 Sturdee Avenue, Rosebank, Johannesburg 2196, South Africa

Penguin Books Ltd, Registered Offices: 80 Strand, London WC2R 0RL, England

Published by Gotham Books, a member of Penguin Group (USA) Inc.

Previously published as a Gotham Books hardcover edition with the title *People Are Idiots and I Can Prove It!*

First trade paperback printing, January 2010

10 9 8 7 6 5 4 3 2 1

Gotham Books and the skyscraper logo are trademarks of Penguin Group (USA) Inc.

Library of Congress Cataloging in Publication data has been applied for

ISBN: 978-1-592-40467-4

Printed in the United States of America
Set in Janson Text, Liteweit, and Niteweit
Designed by Sabrina Bowers

To idiots everywhere.
Without them, I would be unemployed.

> *"No matter how smart you are,*
> *you spend most of your day being an idiot."*
>
> Scott Adams, *The Dilbert Future*

CONTENTS

PREFACE

People are idiots. In this book I point out exactly what people do to prove my point. I do this by following people's actions to show that it is what we **do** that gives us the results we have. I prove that, while we say we want success, happiness, health, financial security, good government and great kids, we don't really do much to make sure it happens. In this way, our actions contradict our words. We sabotage our own success. That is an easy case to make on many levels, and I'm confident you will agree with me as I unfold my thoughts on each of these subjects.

This book is the result of an offhand comment I made during a radio interview where they took calls from the listening audience. I was on a rant talking about my book *You're Broke Because You Want to Be*. I was rattling off some of the stupid things people do with their money to screw up their lives. A listener called in to talk with me and said, "Larry, I get the feeling you think people are idiots." I replied with, "I want to clear up that misconception right now! I do not think people are idiots. I *know* people are idiots and I can prove it."

My comment shocked both the caller and the host of the show. But it did get everyone's attention. I then went on to demonstrate, in just a few short sentences, why I know people are idiots. Those few sentences, which you will read in the upcoming chapters, became the impetus for this book.

I know people are messing up their lives by making stupid decisions and doing stupid things. You know it, too. How can anyone not know it? I have decided it is time to bring the stupidity of people out in the open and address it head-on. I am tired of people pussyfooting around the topic of stupid, idiotic people and my guess is you are, too. I find it laughable that society has become so politically correct that we can no longer call things what they are and have to make up ridiculous excuses for the fact that people are just being idiots. It is time to deal with the stupid things people do, figure out why they do them, and show them how they can stop doing them.

In this book, I will take on business, family, health, obesity, success, money and more. I will point out exactly what changes have to take place in order for people to turn their lives around. I will show you how you can change your results by taking responsibility for your words and your wants and putting some new ideas into action to make it all happen.

This book not only proves how people are idiots and why people are idiots but it also shows exactly what must be done to stop being an idiot. While this book may have a very negative title, I consider it to be my most positive book to date. No other book I have written has more tactical information on exactly what must be done to change results.

What you can expect: a little bit of business. A little personal development. A little finance. A little parenting. A little about relationships. A little health and wellness. Some solid how-tos. Some fun. Plus a whopping dose of attitude and common sense!

MY STUFF VS. OTHER PEOPLE'S STUFF

I regularly work with many other big-time speakers and authors who have maniacal fans who worship them. I have seen these guys walk into a room and watched the crowd become orgasmic with delight from their guru's presence. People stand in their chairs and scream and cry and get goose bumps. Over a self-help guru? Come on.

This is what happened with Rush Limbaugh and his ditto-heads. And what a great name for this type of fan. Dittoheads are people who mindlessly agree on an issue or idea because they are followers of the person who put forth the idea. They have stopped thinking for themselves and allow the guru to think for them. I have seen this a lot with fundamentalist Christians. Jim Bakker had his own version of dittoheads. Lots of people loved Jim and his wife, Tammy Faye, and supported their ministry. Then ol' Jimmy had an affair with a staffer, and his followers discovered he wasn't quite as pure as they thought he was. Their faith was shaken because they lost sight of the message itself and focused too much on the mouthpiece for the message, and he turned out to be a disappointment. There are many extreme examples of the phenomenon, such as the Branch Davidians in Waco and Jim Jones and his followers at Jonestown. Jones's followers ended up drinking the Kool-Aid and died as a result. Now, that is extreme. I recall a great quote attributed to the Buddha that said, "The teacher comes to point the way and the student ends up worshipping the pointer." The focus should be on "the way" and not on the one who points the way. The pointer is just a person—and people always disappoint.

In this book, I am showing you *a way* to become more successful. I don't claim that it is *the* way; it is only *a* way. I show you ways to become successful that have worked for me. I believe they will work for you, too.

I don't want you to drink my Kool-Aid. I am much more interested in you mixing up a batch of your own. I want you to think for yourself. I would like for you to nod your head from time to time in agreement, but I would enjoy it if you vehemently disagreed with me every once in a while, too. If you disagree, it proves you are thinking. Thinking is always a good thing and is very rare, so if this book makes you think, it's a great book.

> *"Many people would sooner die than think;*
> *in fact, they do so."*
> Bertrand Russell

FOR MY NEW READERS WHO ARE NOT FAMILIAR WITH MY WRITING STYLE

I don't like surprises and I doubt you do either. So allow me to comment on my style for those of you who are new to my writing. It is confrontational. (I know that.) It is abrasive. (Again, I'm aware.) A woman wrote a critique of my book *Shut Up, Stop Whining & Get a Life*, saying she didn't like the book after reading it because she found it to be abrasive. Seems to me that the title alone should have been a clue. Did she really have to read the whole book to figure that out? It's like picking up the dictionary and complaining because it's full of definitions. The same applies to this book. The title alone is a warning, but it won't be enough of a warning for some folks, so I am including another: Don't be shocked or surprised by what I say between these pages. You have been warned.

I am also fully aware that some people don't respond well to confrontational and abrasive, and instead respond better to warm and fuzzy. I am not a warm and fuzzy kind of guy. I can't be. I tried it one time and it almost made me throw up. So if warm and fuzzy is what you are comfortable with and enjoy, you probably aren't going to like me.

However, not all of what I say is confrontational and abrasive. It is primarily instructional. In fact, the bulk of this book is instructional. I use a "Wake 'em Up—Shake 'em Up—Point 'em in the Right Direction" approach. Yes, I am confrontational to wake you up. I am also abrasive to shake you up. It's my style and I find that approach is very effective with many people. However, the bulk of what I do is to point people in the right direction. I do that by telling stories, many of which are pretty funny, and by offering detailed action plans for you to follow.

This book starts out abrasive and confrontational. I would call it "Go ugly early." I hit you pretty hard at the beginning. Hard enough to hurt. Hard enough to metaphorically knock you down. If that's all I did, I would just be mean. I'm not mean. I'll knock you down and be glad I did, but I'll be right there to help you back up, point you in the right direction and give you a little boot in the butt to get you going. That's where the instructional part comes in, and that's what the bulk of the book is all about.

As you read the book, you will also discover that I make my point quickly. There is no reason to beat around the bush when it comes to telling people what they need to do to be more successful. Why tell you how to build the watch when I could just tell you what time it is? I don't have time for tact. I am not going to sugarcoat things just to protect your fragile ego or to keep from bruising your delicate sensibilities. I am just going to say, "Stop doing that because it doesn't work, and start doing this because it does." Sound good to you?

You have heard it said before: "Different strokes for different folks." The same applies to self-help advice. Different styles fit different needs. Some people need the warm, sweet, loving, nurturing style in order to change. I am clearly not their guy. Some need a swift kick in the butt to wake them up so they can begin to change because they are sick of living the way they are living. If that's you, then, honey, welcome to my world. We are going to get along just fine!

If we don't click, it's not your fault and it's not my fault. It is because our styles are not in alignment. I won't blame you and you shouldn't blame me. But before you dismiss what I have to say too quickly, realize that becoming uncomfortable as the result of reading my words is not necessarily a bad thing. The truth hurts. One of my favorite quotes is by Werner Erhard, who said, "The truth will set you free but first it will piss you off." If something in this book rubs you the wrong way or pisses you off, that's probably a good thing. It means it is the truth. Or at least it is the truth for you at that moment.

The truth hurts;
that's how you know it's the truth!

I recently received a letter from a woman who had read one of my books. Here are her words:

*You warned me at the beginning of your book that you were blunt. I thought I could take it. I couldn't. I read what you said about being fat, stupid and lazy. It hurt my feelings and then it made me mad. I was mad at you for saying the things I knew were true. I **was** fat, stupid and lazy. So I got mad enough to lose eighty pounds and go back to school. I ended up with a better job, more money and I look fantastic. My whole life is different now. Thanks for saying the words I hated to hear.*

I get many letters very similar to this one. People read my books and get mad at me. I don't believe it is me they are mad at. I don't believe it is my words they are mad at. I believe they are mad because I have stripped away their excuses and forced them to finally confront the real enemy: their own actions. When they confront that enemy, they change. They could have changed at any time in the past, but they didn't. Why? Because we live in a world that encourages us to be victims and remain comfortable with our mediocre results. A world that is okay with being just okay. That is not my world. I honestly want the best for people and I believe people can achieve amazing results once they strip away the BS and get to work. I consider it my job in life to help people strip away the BS and to show them the actions to take to make their lives better. To do my job, I have to make people uncomfortable.

Get ready for a roller coaster of emotions. Be prepared to get mad at me and to get mad at yourself. Mostly get prepared to go to work, because your life is about to change.

SOME GOOD NEWS AND SOME BAD NEWS

This book is a fast read. It won't take you more than a couple of hours to get through the words on the pages. That is the good news. Here is the bad news: This is a workbook. Reading the book alone won't make much of a difference in your life. However, filling out the work sheets will. The work sheets are where you will find the answers to why your life hasn't worked out for you the way you wanted it to. I speak in generalities that apply to most people in most situations. That's because I don't know you. You know you, though. The work sheets will allow you to personalize the process so you can really begin to make progress in your life.

Put in the time. There is no rush to get to the end of the book. Take the few minutes it requires to fill out the lists. Get serious about your success this time.

THE
IDIOT
FACTOR

INTRODUCTION

WHY SUCH AN OBNOXIOUS TITLE?

People tend to have a gut reaction to the messages in my books. Chances are, when you first picked this up and flipped through, you responded in one of two ways: You said either "He's got that right!" or "Who the hell does this guy think he is?" Either way, I got a reaction from you. That was my purpose.

For those of you in the first category who agree with my premise in this book, you probably even said to yourself, "I could have written this book." It seems like we all recognize that people act like idiots, and sabotage their chances for success as a result.

Those of you in the latter category probably think I am rude and arrogant, and that *I* am the idiot for saying other people are idiots. I knew that was going to be the first response from a good number of people when they read the title. They won't like the title, won't buy the book and won't read the book. Yet they will rush home to hop on their computer, where they will go to one of the zillion or so Internet blogs that review books or to the online sites where you can buy books, where they will happily trash both the book and me for even daring to write a book that calls people idiots.

I am way ahead of you on this one because I have been down this road before. So for those of you who have made it this far, I applaud you. You have proven you are open to hearing a unique viewpoint and are willing to learn more of what I have to say. You are giving me a chance to explain my position. I believe everyone deserves the chance to explain themselves if for no other reason than to give you an informed reason to disagree with them. At least by giving me that chance, when you see all of those attacks against me and this book, you will know the truth. You will have an informed opinion. You can then trash the book or praise it all you want. You will have earned the right because you have read it.

SELF-HELP OR *SHELF*-HELP?

Many books never make it off the bookstore shelf. I think it is because they look and sound boring. I believe it is important to get people's attention. To do that, you have to be bold. Bold in what you say or do. Bold in your appearance. If what you have looks like what everyone else has, then it will be considered to be just like what everyone else has. Make sense to you?

I am fairly bold in the way I dress. (Did he just say *fairly*?) You did see the cover, didn't you? I wear brightly colored, sequined cowboy shirts and custom cowboy boots. I have a shaved head and a strange little Amish-style goatee. I wear earrings and enough jewelry to open a jewelry store at a moment's notice with just what I'm wearing. I don't look like your typical self-help guru. That's okay; my advice isn't typical either. When I appear on one of the national television shows talking about money and there is a panel of experts all in suits, with one person looking much like the next, there I am sticking out like the proverbial sore thumb. Do people respond to my appearance? Of course they do. One guy wrote a critique saying, "How can you take financial advice from someone who dresses like a rodeo clown?"

That made me laugh! Most people applaud that I have the guts to dress the way I want. I get letters from people saying, "I wish I could do that!" I speak to Fortune 500 companies that want to make sure I wear all of my garb and even ask if I'll wear my sunglasses onstage when I speak. But like it or hate it, people recognize it and remember it. It's bold. It gets noticed. I dress boldly and I make bold statements in both my speaking and my writing. That boldness carries over to the titles of my books as well.

There are lots of books with titles like *The Ten Keys to Success* and *The Secrets to Attracting What You Want*. You have seen them just as I have. Safe little books with safe little titles that try to convince you that you can do anything if you will only believe! I think people are tired of that worn-out approach and are more sophisticated than to buy into the same old motivational mumbo jumbo that has been said over and over in the same way so many times. I believe most people see a title like that and say to themselves, "Same old crap from some do-gooder motivational guy." For the most part, they are correct. Consequently, the book just sits on the shelf and gathers dust. While the book might actually contain some life-changing information, it simply doesn't matter, because people won't read it since it looks and sounds boring! What difference does it make whether a book is good or how great the information is inside the book if no one ever picks it up, buys it and reads it? I have learned that basic truth with all of my books: Titles attract attention. So selfishly and from a marketing standpoint, it is a good idea to get people's attention. Once you have their attention, you can begin to teach them something. But a closed book on a shelf in a bookstore or in a library doesn't teach anyone anything, regardless of how good the information inside might be. The fact that you are reading this book proves that it is no longer shelf-help.

My purpose in this book is to challenge you. I like to challenge people. When people feel challenged, they work harder. They have something to prove, even if it is just to prove the other guy wrong. I want you to be challenged in this book to work harder on your life so you can actually have all the things you *say* you want to have.

IN THE MIDDLE OR ON THE EDGE

In every area of life and business, the people on the edge are the ones who have made history. No one who comes from the centrist position—that safe middle ground—ever really had much of an impact on society. It's the people on the edge we all know and remember. Elvis and the Beatles: musicians on the edge. Pablo Picasso and Salvador Dalí: artists on the edge. The United States of America would not exist if it weren't for a handful of renegades. Benjamin Franklin, Thomas Jefferson and George Washington were all edgy guys. Jesus was definitely on the edge. Gandhi was on the edge. Good or bad, right or wrong, it doesn't matter. The people who change history are not the people who do the safe things, take the easy route, follow the status quo or say what everyone else says or try to make everyone happy.

I am not claiming to be Elvis, Picasso, Gandhi or Jesus. I am just a guy who has moved away from the center to offer you a unique, edgier approach to personal development. This approach can move you and your results from the middle to the edge.

The multitudes live in the middle, living mediocre lives, thinking mediocre thoughts, doing mediocre things and achieving mediocre results. Their income falls in the median range. Their houses are in the median range. Their entire lives are median, mediocre and stuck deeply in the middle. Sadly, most don't even recognize their predicament because everyone they know is stuck there in the middle with them.

WHAT IS THE PURPOSE OF THIS BOOK?

My goal is to get you unstuck from that comfortable mediocre lifestyle and move you to the edge. The edge is where only a few of us live. The edge is where people dare to defy their upbringing, their education and their situation to become wildly happy, successful and prosperous in spite of themselves. The edge is the place you get to live once you stop lying to yourself and everyone else and squarely face where you are, and then decide to go to a better place. The edge is where the fun is, where the money is and where true self-satisfaction is. The best part of living on the edge is that it isn't crowded at all.

I wrote this book to get people's attention and remind them they are living lives contradictory to what they say they want. To prove to people that they are lying to themselves when they only *say* they want success, happiness and prosperity. To make people aware that their results are the results of their actions. To show people they are sabotaging their own success and to show them exactly what they have to do to turn their lives around.

WHAT YOU CAN EXPECT FROM THIS BOOK

You can expect solutions. That's what I have to offer here: simple, action-based solutions to life's situations. If I didn't give you solutions, this book would just be a long rant about the ills of society. What good would come from that? My goal is to present the problems and to offer simple, action-based solutions to fix them.

I have included lists of exactly what people can do to change their lives in just about any area. I give a mini action plan for success for each. I say "mini action plan" because there is no possible way to give you a complete list of every single thing you are going to need to do to become completely successful in each area of your life. Nor can I provide you with a list that will fit each and every situation of your specific predicament. Instead, I will give you a short list that can be used to get you started on the right track to turn your life around. My lists will cover several common situations that most people face. The action lists are the power and the purpose of this little book and are my formula for success.

NOTHING NEW HERE

One of the criticisms I often receive about my books is that they contain a considerable amount of simplicity, or what I call "The Duh Factor." People say things like "Nothing new here." My response: "Thank you." There is nothing new out there when it comes to success, happiness and prosperity. Those books that promise you a brand-new approach to success are lying to you. Beware the person who says, "I've got some brand-new stuff for you." Walk away with the confidence that you are leaving another idiot in your dust. There is no "brand-new stuff." There are medical breakthroughs. There are scientific breakthroughs. There are no personal development breakthroughs. No one is coming up with any brand-new keys to success. It's not going to happen. The people who tell you otherwise are playing on your weaknesses because you think the old stuff hasn't worked for you so far, so maybe something new will. Then they repackage the old stuff and call it new and improved to sucker you into buying it. Remember New Coke? It was a brilliant marketing ploy to take up more shelf space in the grocery store. It worked for a while because people always rush to buy anything "new and improved." Eventually it fizzled because people realized that you can't improve on the original formula. That's the way it works with personal development and business advice, too.

People always rush to buy what is packaged as "new and improved," but eventually it goes away and people return to the original formula.

My stuff is the original formula. I want you to know that what I talk about is old stuff. Old stuff that just about every successful person has done. Stuff that works. Stuff that is proven. Stuff that hasn't changed for eons and won't ever change. Stuff you can count on. What it takes to be successful today is exactly what it has taken for centuries. Please don't expect any new information from me, because I don't have any. It's the same old stuff every true philosopher of success has covered for hundreds of years. You are just getting my personal spin on it—the Larry-ized version.

A guy wrote me a nasty letter about my books, saying that I didn't have one thing to offer that wasn't plain old common sense. He is totally right. But I have found that common sense, like common knowledge and common courtesy, is anything but common. If you read my ideas and say, "That's plain old common sense," you won't get any argument from me.

I have also gotten feedback saying that everyone already knows all of the stuff I talk about. I wish that were true. It isn't. I will agree that everyone *should* know this stuff, but that just isn't the case. Even if I am wrong on this one and everyone does know it, they don't do it. It comes down to what I believe about knowledge that contradicts the old maxim "Knowledge Is Power." Sorry, that isn't true. Knowledge is *not* power. The *implementation* of knowledge is power. What you know makes little or no difference in your life. What you *do* with what you know makes all the difference in the world.

> *Knowledge is NOT power.*
> *The implementation of knowledge is power.*

These are my principles:

Your life is your own damn fault.

■

Take responsibility for it.

■

Learn what you need to do to fix it.

■

Take action on what you've learned.

■

Enjoy the results.

That's about all it takes to be happy, successful and prosperous. Pretty simple, huh? I don't apologize for having just a few principles. I don't believe success is all that complicated. I hit these few ideas over and over again in many different ways. I talk about how they work in different situations. I say them in different ways. I do that because at the end of this book, I want there to be no question about my position and what you need to do to be more successful. I want you to hear these ideas so many times in so many different ways that you will internalize them completely.

Repetition is the key to internalization.

A LAST THOUGHT BEFORE YOU BEGIN

This is not a book on the *philosophy* of success. This is a book about the practical application of success. It is a call to action. My goal for you is to read this book, then lay it aside, get off your butt and do something!

SECTION ONE

THE IDIOT FACTOR

CHAPTER ONE

YOU SAID YOU COULD PROVE IT; OKAY, PROVE IT!

Drive down any street in the world for ten minutes and watch the way people drive and there will be no doubt people are idiots.

Walk through any mall and watch people spending money and look at what they are buying and you will know people are idiots.

Sit in the parking lot of any fast-food restaurant (please just sit in the parking lot and save yourself the calories by not going in) and observe how fat the people are who are eating there, and there will be no question that people are idiots.

Those three things alone should prove my point. But what fun would it be to stop there? Let's get more specific, and as I love to say, "It's about to get ugly!"

MORE WAYS PEOPLE ARE IDIOTS

Health

■ You have heard the statement Life Is Short. Yet people make conscious choices every day to shorten their lives even more by smoking cigarettes, eating more than they should and remaining sedentary. Is that idiotic? I'm guessing the right answer would be yes.

■ Well over 300,000 adult deaths in the United States each year are attributable to unhealthy eating habits, physical inactivity or sedentary behavior.

■ More than 60 percent of adults are not regularly active and 25 percent are not active at all. Less than 20 percent of high school students are active for more than twenty minutes per day.

■ Americans spend $33 billion annually on weight-loss products and services. Wouldn't it be a lot cheaper to just eat less and go for a walk? People complain that they have no money—I could save society $33 billion a year in this area alone.

■ People say they want to live long healthy lives, yet 1.3 billion people light up cigarettes every day. And every cigarette you smoke shortens your life by thirteen minutes.

■ Every day, people choose to eat things that will shorten their lives. The average daily caloric intake of an American is more than 3,300 calories. Yet the recommended number of calories is 2,500 for a male and 1,900 for a female. People are fat primarily because they eat like idiots. I just read a study that said if we continue at our current "growth" rate, in twenty years, 86 percent of Americans will be obese.

A rant. Doctors are idiots in this area as well, even though they have spent years in medical school learning exactly what it takes to be healthy. People go to overweight doctors who smoke to find out how to be healthy. Does that really make sense? You are an idiot if you go to a doctor who is choosing to destroy his own health. "Fat doctor" equals "lousy doctor" in my mind. A doctor who smokes cigarettes should be stripped of his medical license. Licensing a doctor who violates such a basic tenet of being healthy makes as much sense as passing out day-care certificates to convicted sex offenders. Avoid doctors who are fat, who smoke, who automatically think that drugs and surgery are the first answer to everything that ails you and who make you wait more than thirty minutes to see them.

I want my doctor to look like Clark Kent and be Superman underneath his white smock, or Wonder Woman if it's a female doctor. I want them to be fit and healthy. Ironically, if you ever want to see a gathering of overweight people, go into a hospital, clinic or doctor's office and look at the employees. Interesting that the health care profession attracts so many fat people. You would think that if there were ever a group of people who would know better, it would be health care professionals. Wait—they must be idiots, too!

Parenting

■ People say they want great kids. Of course they say that; who doesn't want to raise good kids? But the reality is that the average amount of time parents spend in meaningful conversation with their children is three and one-half minutes per week. Three and one-half minutes! Two hundred ten seconds per week. Thirty seconds per day. Sure, we want good kids, just not enough to talk to them. This one should make you mad or ill or both.

■ People say they want good public schools for their kids. Yet only a small percentage of parents belong to or attend PTA meetings or go to parent-teacher conferences.

■ Twenty-five percent of teenage girls have an STD. Parents . . . where are you? A little good parenting might be in order here to teach kids what causes this stuff! We might even teach this in the school system, but we would never dare let a school teach sex education, would we?

■ The number of obese children is staggering and growing every day. Thirty percent of children six to nineteen years of age are either overweight or at risk of being obese. Don't blame anyone but parents for this one. The parents pay for the food and put it on the table, or should I say put it in front of the television? The parents are the ones driving the kids to the fast-food restaurants. The parents are the ones sticking French fries in the face of a toddler and thinking they have just fed their child.

A rant. Your kids are your fault. You set the example for them. If they are fat, it's your fault. If they are lazy, it's your fault. If they don't study, it's your fault. You have control over them. They belong to you and are your total responsibility. You are the adult and he or she is the child. You are the leader and the manager and the boss. Keep that chain of command in mind. You must set the example for them to follow. Here's a clue next time you wonder why your kids are the way they are: Look in the mirror. Your kids always reflect the behavior you have shown them to be acceptable. Your kids are little versions of you.

Finances

■ People sign contracts with credit companies, agreeing to pay their bill on a certain date. While the print is small, the rules and regulations are clearly laid out in black and white—all you have to do is read them. Then people don't make their payments on time and don't pay the minimum amount as they agreed (probably because they spent their money at the mall or eating out). Why are these people surprised when their interest rate goes up and the company reports their late payment to the credit bureaus and their credit score goes down? The penalties for not paying on time or making the minimum payment were clearly laid out. The credit card company was only keeping its word. Perhaps those people should do the same and keep their word to the credit card company. Because credit card companies keep their word, they are labeled "predatory."

■ By the way, there is never a need to have more than three credit cards. You don't need to open a store credit card to save 10 percent on today's purchase. That's a great trick that makes you think you are saving 10 percent, but the reality is that you now have one more credit card at a high interest rate that will reflect on your credit rating. Forget the 10 percent savings and realize you don't need another credit card. Besides, when you buy something at 40 percent off, you aren't saving 40 percent. You are spending 60 percent. Don't be an idiot. If you weren't planning on buying it at full price, you aren't saving anything.

■ Another example: The average cost of a wedding today is almost $30,000. Yet those couples who spend that much on the wedding (or have that much spent for them on the wedding) rarely have enough money to make a down payment on a house. How smart is that? Seems like your future would be more secure by investing in a home than in a twenty-minute wedding. Am I against weddings? No, weddings are great. But don't sacrifice your future for one good day.

■ In recent years, people bought houses on interest-only loans. They could barely afford the interest and definitely could not afford both the interest and the principal. Guess that's why they took the interest-only loan in the first place. They were told that at some point, their payment would go up and they would be responsible for both the interest and the principal. They signed a contract saying they understood. When it happened, they discovered they couldn't afford to make the new payment. Who got the blame? The lender. Again, the lender got labeled as predatory. The only appropriate label in the transaction is

STUPID, and that label goes to the borrower. Come on. Read your contract.

■ The average fifty-year-old in America has less than $2,500 saved. Let's say you go to work when you are twenty-five. (Most people go to work much earlier than that, but I will keep the math easy for you.) You went to work at twenty-five and you are now fifty years old. In twenty-five years, you have been able to save only $2,500? One hundred dollars a year is the best you could do? $8.33 per month is all you could manage to put away? You just couldn't seem to do much better than $2 per week? Dear Mr. or Mrs. Average Fifty-Year-Old, you are an idiot!

■ The economy sucks. People say they can't afford gasoline or milk. Houses are in foreclosure. Yet the tables in Vegas, Reno, Atlantic City and all of the other places with legalized gambling are so crowded, you can barely find a seat. Ninety-nine percent of the people who gamble cannot afford to lose a dime yet willingly pay to travel to a place to gamble away their house payment. Idiots!

■ People buy extended warranties on appliances and electronics. Folks, things don't break down like they used to and when they do, you will probably find it cheaper to replace the product with a new one. The new one will do more than the old one and it will probably cost less than the extended warranty did.

■ People give money to people collecting door-to-door for charities. Reputable charities do not send kids to camp by putting people on the street to ask you for money and all you have to do is buy magazines to make it happen. Sucker!

■ People buy bottles of 3,300-calorie flavored water. In fact, let's take this to the basic level of stupidity: bottled water, period. It has been proven that regular tap water is just as pure as bottled water. In fact, we are now seeing a rise in tooth decay in children because bottled water lacks fluoride. Plus, the bottles are not good for the environment. If you are drinking bottled water for convenience, then get one good bottle and fill it from the tap.

People who purchase crap from TV commercials are idiots.

■ The Infinity Razor—"the last razor you will ever buy." Have you seen this commercial? You buy this one razor and it will last you for the rest of your life. Though you do get a second one for only half price. Question: Why do you need a second one if you only need one for the rest of your life? If you actually think that this one razor is going to last the rest of your entire life, you are either an idiot or you are planning to die next week.

■ "You can lose weight without changing your diet or doing any exercise." Products that make this claim make millions from infomercials. If you think that a pill, cream or potion is going to help you lose weight without any dieting or exercise, you are an idiot!

■ "You can grow new hair." You're kidding, right? Or how about this one: Spray paint for your bald spot. Oh, yeah, that's a good idea. No one is going to notice the paint on your head.

■ "You can look ten years younger if you will just rub on this special super-duper anti-aging cream." Ladies, you are suckers when you buy this stuff. No cream is going to make you look ten years younger.

■ Some of the worst crap out there is pretty much *anything* sold on television for $19.95. Can you say "Pocket Fisherman"?

A rant. Most people don't have money to do the things that matter because they are spending the money on things that don't matter. The things most people consider "necessities" are in reality "luxuries." When I tell people to live within their means, they often respond with, "But, Larry, can't I have any fun?" Sure you can. Try having all of your bills and obligations paid on time, with money in the bank, money invested, and savings for your kids' college and your retirement, then tell me how much fun that is.

Business

■ People start their own companies and go into business for themselves when they have never read a book on how to start a company or keep one in business. Some basic business knowledge might come in handy if you're trying to run a business, don't you think? Sales down? Have you read any sales books? Customer service suck? There are only about ten thousand books out there on how to deliver better customer service. Have you read any of them?

■ I am amazed that so many people don't seem to have basic skills like grammar and spelling. I regularly get e-mails from people who must have typed with their elbows. No one could hit that many wrong keys with their fingers. Do people not have spell-check? Come on. When you type a word and your computer highlights it in red, it is a clue that it might need some work! Pet peeves of mine: *your* instead of *you're*, and *there* instead of *their*. And the funny thing is, spell-check probably won't catch these.

■ People don't return phone calls in a timely manner. I have friends who are busy people—rich people—people with more work and other things going on in their lives than they have free time. They return their phone calls. I don't know of anyone any busier than I am, and I return my phone calls. Yet there are people who don't have one damn thing going on in their lives and they just can't seem to find the time to return their calls. They are idiots. Plus, they are rude. Rude idiots.

■ Voice mail. It is primarily used as a way to avoid answering your phone calls. What bothers me most about voice mail is when people have so many messages in their mailbox that it won't accept any more. At least you know when that happens, you are not getting a call back.

■ People say they want job security, they want a promotion, they want to be respected at work or they want a raise. Yet they show up late and put in minimum effort. Not a great way to achieve job security and advancement.

A rant. Businesses exist for one reason and only one reason: to make a profit. The most profitable companies serve their customers well. They assure their profitability by employing people who are worth more than they cost. If your business isn't doing well, it's because you aren't doing these things.

General idiotic behavior

■ People go to the drive-in bank window without being prepared. They wait until they are at the window to start filling out their deposit slip while holding up an entire line of cars. Did these bozos just suddenly remember why they were at the bank? Didn't they know they would need to have a deposit slip filled out? And when your transaction is completed . . . move! Don't fiddle around in your purse or put your stuff in the glove compartment. Move! The people behind you have lives and we would like to get on with them.

■ People park in spaces reserved for the disabled. I recently pointed out to a guy that he had just parked in a disabled space.

He said, "Hey, it's been a tough day." I said, "It would have been a lot tougher if you were really disabled. But maybe fat, stupid and lazy counts now." He was so taken aback that he just sputtered, got in his car and drove away.

■ People drink and drive, get in an accident and then want to sue the bar and the bartender for over-serving them. People spill hot coffee in their lap and sue the people who made the coffee hot. Yet if the coffee weren't hot, they would complain about that. Stop suing people because you are clumsy or because you don't know when you've had enough!

■ People say they want a great relationship with their spouse or significant other, yet a recent study said that 65 percent of people spend more time with their computers than with their spouses. Why is that? Is it because their computer gives them more companionship? Or better sex? Ouch! I actually said that! Most people make very little effort to look good or smell good or to have a conversation with their spouse. They crawl into bed with bad breath, smelling like a goat, and then gripe about the fact that their spouse doesn't want to have sex with them.

■ People with no job and nothing but time on their hands have dirty houses, filthy cars and overgrown yards. Why? It's not like they have a job to go to that takes all their time!

■ The average American reads at a seventh-grade level. You would think that the biggest, brightest and best country in the world could turn out smarter people, wouldn't you? The truth is, we are not the brightest country. We don't rank number one in anything except consumption. American students are well below international averages in math and science. Forty percent of high school students have not mastered what they need to know at a given grade level. That doesn't seem to matter much, because they still pass and move on to the next grade. We have high school graduates who cannot read their own diploma.

■ The human race is knowingly destroying the environment. We pretend there is nothing we can do about it, and that makes us all idiots. I am not going to make this a "green" point, so calm down. But couldn't we just recycle as a bare-minimum effort to help the planet out a bit?

■ People see crimes happening and politely turn their heads while people are beaten up, run over and even raped. I watched a television report recently where people in a park walked right past a group of juveniles destroying a car. It was all staged to check whether people would become involved. Dozens of people walked by for hours, and only one called the police or confronted the juveniles. When the people were later asked why they didn't do anything to intervene, one of the popular answers was, "It wasn't my car." Disgusting.

■ People spend millions of dollars every year on psychics. Come on, people . . . psychics! No one can predict your future except you. Take control of your own future and stop spending money with these frauds.

■ People ask for advice—even beg for advice. It seems they will do anything for advice. They will even pay for advice. Then they won't *take* the advice. Idiots. Your doctor will tell you exactly what to do to be healthier. Will you do it? Probably not. You obviously know better than any stupid doctor who went to medical school for eight years. You will do what you think is right, whether you know what you are talking about or not. People will go to a rich guy for advice on what it takes to be rich. The rich guy tells them exactly what to do. Do they do it? Nope. I get asked all the time what people need to do to become successful. I used to tell people what to do. I would work with them and explain step-by-step what they needed to do. Did they do it? Very few ever did a thing. I'm thinking of writing a book called *Why Bother; You Won't Do It Anyway!*

■ People say they want better government, yet only 60 percent of the people who could vote are actually registered to vote. Historically, only half of those who are registered to vote and can vote actually vote. Do people really want better government? Sure they do, just not enough to vote. I recently wrote a blog about voting on my Web site. I found it amazing that people responded by saying that voting made no difference and that we don't live in a democracy anyway so it was all a waste of time. I guess their goal was just to piss me off. Vote! It's a privilege that must be exercised. I vote to change things. I vote because I'm interested. However, I vote for one reason more than any other: I want the right to gripe. If you don't vote, you don't have the right to complain. Never lose the right to complain.

■ People say that they want honesty from their government officials and yet nearly 20 percent of taxpayers cheat on their taxes.

A few short ones that prove people are idiots

$300 jeans.

The lottery. Your chance of winning is about 1 in 176 million.

Turn signals. They haven't come as an option on automobiles for a long time. So why do people use them only optionally?

Chain letters. These days they come as chain e-mails. "Break the chain and you will experience bad luck." The only bad luck involved is in knowing someone stupid enough to send you a chain letter.

"You can get rich quick." Yeah, right. No rich person would ever agree with that one! Wealth comes pretty slowly unless you win the lottery, and I've already established the statistics on that. Go to work instead.

If I can hear your car stereo while sitting in my car, you are an idiot.

Ginsu anything.

Transportation Security Administration, or TSA. For anyone who travels a lot, that's all that needs to be said on that one.

If you are chowing down on a 3,000-calorie meal of a double bacon cheeseburger with a boatload of chili-cheese fries, ordering a diet cola or light beer doesn't really make much sense, does it?

The clincher

Seven percent of society believes Elvis is still alive. Yep, people are indeed idiots.

THE BIGGEST PROOF OF ALL THAT PEOPLE ARE IDIOTS

If you don't read anything else, read this one!

Human beings are the only species on Earth who knowingly choose to be less than they have the potential for being. No other living thing in nature chooses to be less than it could be. Only people do that. People choose to die earlier than they have to by living an unhealthy lifestyle. People choose to earn less than they could. People choose to destroy the environment they live in. People choose to be sedentary and not develop physically as much as they could. No other creature chooses to underdevelop and not reach its full potential. Did you ever see a tree grow to about six feet tall and say, "Eh, I'm good right here," and then stop growing? No, a tree grows to be as tall as it can be. A tree grows as many leaves as it can. A tree puts down as many roots as it can. A tree bears as much fruit as it possibly can. Trees continue to grow and produce as long as they are alive.

All plants grow to be as big as they can be. The same applies to every other living thing on Earth. Rats, horses, pigs and dogs all grow as much as they can. Fish and worms and amoebas all do the same. Every living species grows, develops and produces as much as it possibly can. Everything except people. People are the only species in the universe that chooses to be less than it can be. They get to a point in their lives and just stop. They choose to quit learning, quit growing and quit developing. They choose to quit earning, quit being productive and quit contributing. People stop because they choose to stop, not because they have to, need to or should. It is a choice.

This alone should be enough proof for you that people are idiots. This one profound concept should make you pause and think, "This guy is dead-on right." If you had never considered this thought before, you could toss the book aside right now and you would have received your money's worth.

You can argue about everything else I say in this book, but on this one you must concede. People choose to be less. Period. I do. You do. I choose every day to do less than I could. You choose every day to do less, be less and have less than you could have. Just knowing this should make you committed to changing your life.

Let's get personal.

I will bet after you got into my list of why people are idiots, you came up with another ten or so I didn't mention. That's how it seems to work. Once I begin to prove people are idiots, others say, "Larry, you forgot about those people who . . ." The reality is, we all know others who are being idiots and screwing up their own lives as well as inconveniencing the rest of us!

Are you innocent? Ask yourself whether you've said some of the following things:

I want more money.

I want a better relationship with my spouse.

I want good, responsible kids.

I want a promotion.

I want to be healthy.

I want to live a long time.

I want to be happy.

I want to retire.

I want better government.

I want to be smarter.

I want, I want, I want. . . .

Statements like these seem to be about all I hear from people. Frankly, I am sick of it. People say they want these things and it's simply not true. In fact, it is a big ugly lie.

Total BS

You don't want any of those things you say you want. Those are just words. You want what you have. That's why you have it. If you wanted something different, you would have something different. Or you would at least be taking action to get something different from what you have. You have been living a lie, and it's time you took a good hard look at the truth. The truth is that your life is the way you want it to be.

Success is simple once you understand this basic concept. Your life is the way it is because of the actions you have taken. Your actions produced your results. Nothing else. Not your words and certainly not your wants. It was your actions. This point cannot be argued. You don't *think* your way to success, regardless of what the new age gurus tell you. You can contemplate success all you want and your life won't change. It is always going to come down to the actions you take.

You have been taking action to bring about what you don't want. That's the life you are living right now. My suggestion is that you start taking action to bring about the life you do want. Stop talking about what you want. I'm tired of hearing it. Your friends and family are tired of hearing it. The whole world is tired of hearing it. Most of all, you should be tired of hearing it. You should be sick of saying it. And you should be disgusted with the results you have decided to settle for.

Don't ever again talk about what you want. It is a waste of words and energy. Instead, simply show me what you *have* and I'll prove to you what you really want. You want what your actions are giving you.

Whoa! You aren't being fair!

No whoa! This is all perfectly fair. I haven't said anything that isn't true and you know it. Just because I call a spade a spade doesn't mean that you need to get defensive. Maybe this is one of those times I warned you about, when the truth hurts.

Besides, my attacks—and yes, they are attacks—are not personal. I never attack people—I attack people's behavior.

But understand this, too: While I am attacking behavior, a person's behavior is an indication of the kind of person he is. If you consistently act in ways that are irresponsible, then you are an irresponsible person. I won't attack you, but I will attack your irresponsibility. To commit one act of being irresponsible is forgivable, especially if you take responsibility and ask forgiveness. Even the most responsible people mess up from time to time. However, consistent irresponsible behavior is the act of an irresponsible person.

"My mama always said, stupid is as stupid does."
Forrest Gump

Not *total* BS

Okay, maybe I went too far by saying that wanting a better life is total BS. I actually do believe people want more success than they are experiencing. These aren't just words we say to make ourselves feel better. I think that, deep down, people honestly, passionately, desperately want more success, happiness and prosperity. They want to be able to do more, be more and have more. The problem is, they have been lulled into thinking that their life is the way it is because of fate, or karma or worse: Their life and results are someone else's fault.

People turn on their televisions and are seduced into victimhood by the reports they see on the news. Obviously the credit card companies, mortgage companies, banks, oil companies, grocery stores and retailers are the reasons people are broke and unsuccessful. People listen to the radio and hear the bankruptcy attorneys say they can rescue you because your financial situation is not your fault at all. People have friends who tell them it is a cold, cruel world out there, and it's no wonder they are having problems. It is so soothing to hear from any source that your pitiful life isn't your own fault . . . and there is the seduction. We will do damn near anything to keep from having to accept that we cause our lives to be the way they are. We cling to the idea that maybe it is someone else's fault that we are unhappy, unsuccessful, sick and broke. Please let it be someone else's fault! PLEASE!

The truth is that people really do want the success they talk about. They want more money, better health, better kids and all the things they say they want. However, their own stupid thinking has convinced them that just saying it will make it happen. Saying it alone will *not* make it happen. Saying what you want only increases the want; it doesn't create the reality. Action turns your wants into reality.

Larry Winget: idiot extraordinaire

Yep, I am an idiot, too. Many times I have made the statement that I could be the poster child for stupidity. I have made every mistake you can think of. I have wrecked my business, gone bankrupt, nearly ruined my marriage, been a lousy parent, wasted time, done stupid things, said stupid things, overspent, underearned, and on and on and on. I constantly do things that contradict what I say I want. I am lazy. I offer myself and others excuses. It is a never-ending list. I add to that list daily. I'm a mess!

A man once wrote a critique of me, saying, "Why would you listen to this guy? He admits he has made all kinds of mistakes and that he doesn't know all it takes to be successful. He says that he only knows what he knows from reading thousands of books on success and from making stupid mistakes." He assumed that was a criticism, when I actually considered it to be a compliment. I am just a regular guy who makes stupid decisions, does stupid things and does his best to learn from them. I share what I have learned from correcting my own mistakes and from reading more than four thousand books so others won't have to go through what I have been through. I speak and write from both a depth of experience and research. I am exactly the guy you should listen to because I have been where most people have been—and gotten past it.

The key to growing is to become aware of your own stupidity. Everyone is stupid. We are all idiots from time to time. I never met anyone who didn't do stupid things. The key is not just to admit being an idiot but also to become aware of when you are being an idiot so you can head it off at the pass before you screw things up too much.

In this way, life is like golf. Few golfers, even the great ones, hit the fairway all the time. Few hit a high percentage of greens. What I find amazing about golf is, there aren't that many really great golf shots off the tee. But golf is not about hitting a great initial shot. Golf is about hitting great correcting shots after you hit a bad shot. The best golfers know how to hit a great correcting shot when they've hit a bad one.

While I'm not that good at hitting great correcting shots in my golf game, I've become pretty good at hitting great correcting shots in my life. That probably is the result of all the practice I have given myself.

When I am not getting the results I want, I try to become aware of why it's happening. Every time, it is because I have done something stupid. I have acted in a way that is inconsistent with my words and my wants. No exception—it is always my fault. I know that about myself. I hate it, but at least I know it. Knowing it and being aware of it allow me to move faster when it comes to fixing it. That is the key. You fix it, and fix it fast, so you don't have to experience the pain of your own stupidity for very long.

You're probably thinking, "Larry, how do I do this?" That's what this book will show you.

But, Larry, life is hard!

Okay, let's get this argument dealt with and out of the way so we can begin to make some progress. Life is hard. I know how hard life is. I know how hard your life is because my life is hard, too.

All anyone has to do to find out how hard life is, is to turn on the TV or pick up a newspaper. Every media source out there will tell you how hard your life is. They will even warn you about how much harder your life is going to get. I know this because I watch television and I read newspapers and magazines. I also read the thousands of e-mails people send me outlining their personal, professional and financial problems. I get it from all sides just like you do—life is indeed very hard for everyone. Like you, I wake up every day and face my own set of problems. They aren't the same problems you face, but they are real to me just like yours are real to you.

We are all faced with hardships. No one is immune to the hardships of life. Never become so self-absorbed as to think life isn't hard for all of us.

Just because you are rich doesn't mean that your life isn't hard. It is just hard in different ways from those who are broke. More zeroes do not make your life problem-free. You just have problems with more zeroes.

Just because you are healthy doesn't mean your life isn't hard. It is just hard in different ways from those who are sick.

Just because you are employed doesn't mean that your life isn't hard. It is just hard in different ways from those who don't have jobs.

Just because your relationship is in a good place now doesn't mean your relationship isn't hard, hasn't been hard or will not at some point be hard.

Just because your kids are on the right track today doesn't mean they aren't going to mess up or be a challenge for you tomorrow.

All of us are faced with the challenges of a complicated society. All of us deal with aging parents, kids who mess up, relationship woes, death, sickness, money, the price of gasoline, guilt, worry, stress and more.

I agree. I'm with you on all of this. Just slow down a minute and consider this:

If life is hard (and I agree that it is), why make it harder than it is already? Why knowingly do things that complicate your life more than it has to be? Why sabotage yourself?

CHAPTER TWO

WHY PEOPLE ARE IDIOTS

or The Ten Ways People Sabotage Their Success

You bought this book because you want to be more success-ful. Everyone wants that. I want it. What people don't un-derstand is that success doesn't come by getting more of anything. I know that may come as a shock and a disappoint-ment. But that's just how it works.

You already have what it takes to be successful. Success comes by giving up some of what you already have. The prob-lem is, you have cluttered up your life with things that keep you from experiencing success. You have to get rid of those things.

Success is a process of elimination. You must eliminate the nonsuc-cessful behaviors to make room for the successful behaviors. To do that, you have to identify the things that are keeping you from being successful.

In the past, I have said that there are only three reasons people aren't successful:

People are stupid.

People are lazy.

People don't give a damn.

Time has changed my view on the three reasons people aren't successful. I've had a few additional years of dealing with stupidity and analyzing why people don't reach their goals and are broke, unhappy, unhealthy and unsuccessful . . . pretty much UN-everything. I've also had more personal contact with a lot more un-everything people and listened to their whining and excuses. After considerable thought about how people get in the way of their own success, I have expanded my list from my basic three to ten.

The Ten Ways People Sabotage Their Success

People are ignorant.

People are stupid.

People are lazy.

People don't give a damn.

People lack vision.

People have low expectations.

People don't recognize the consequences of their actions.

People have bad habits.

People have poor role models.

People have no plan.

PEOPLE ARE IGNORANT.

Being ignorant is the only one of my ten ways people sabotage themselves that is forgivable. It's the only one you aren't totally responsible for, up to a point. Ignorance, by my definition, means you don't know what it takes to do something, be something or have something. You are unaware. You are either uneducated or you simply don't know any better. To tell someone he or she is ignorant is offensive to most people. By my definition, it doesn't have to be offensive. We are all born ignorant. That's not our fault. We don't have any information. We are a blank slate waiting for information to show up so we can start to make informed decisions.

At birth, the decisions are pretty easy: I'm sleepy. I'm hungry. I have a stomachache. Once we got the information to learn how to satisfy that set of needs, we moved to a new level. We went from hunger and sleep to walking and talking. Then we got a little older and we were ignorant about other things. There was a time when we didn't know how to add or subtract. We didn't know our ABCs. Then we learned and our lives changed. But for a while, we were ignorant of these things. As we got older, the things we were ignorant about changed. We didn't know about history or business or how to use a computer. As we got more information and our blank slate got more filled in, our ignorance decreased and we began to make more sophisticated decisions because we had more information.

There was a time when I was ignorant about traveling. A time when I didn't know which fork to use or which side the bread plate was on. A time when I didn't know how to play golf. A time when I didn't know anything about wine. A time when I thought gravy was a food group. I was ignorant about many things. I learned about each of these things and again my life changed. There are still many things I don't have a clue about: things I am truly ignorant about, but I'm working on it. I spend a portion of every day trying to cut down on the number of things I am ignorant about.

There are some things you can remain ignorant about forever and it probably won't matter. I don't think I am ever going to need to know the details of the Byzantine Empire. For some people, that would be critical knowledge; for me, not so much. Being ignorant about things that have nothing to do with your success isn't so bad, but being ignorant about the things that matter is inexcusable. You can't afford to be ignorant about money, business, parenting, life, your health or your success.

It's okay to be ignorant for a while.

You can get by being ignorant for a while. You can last a short time without the correct information and get by by saying, "I don't know." (By the way, saying that you don't know when you really don't know is better than pretending you do know when you don't have a clue.) You can even explain away some of your failures by saying, "I didn't know any better."

So you can get by for a while without knowing. Not for long, but for a while. Actually, there are people who go their entire lives not knowing much of anything. You see these people every day. They are related to you, live next to you or sit in the cubicle right beside you. They are shuffling ignorantly through life with no clue as to why they are having such a hard time.

If you aren't convinced, just turn on your television. Watch Jay Leno interview people on the street, asking them the name of the vice president of the United States or in what city the White House is located, and they don't know. Some of these people are so stupid that Jay turns them into celebrities and uses them often on *The Tonight Show*, showcasing their ignorance. I think these idiots are funny, too, but mostly I hate them for being so stupid.

Wake up!

There comes a point when every person needs to stop pleading ignorance and figure out on his or her own what it takes to really get ahead. Come on! Pay attention. Look around and watch what other people are doing and get a clue about what works and what doesn't work.

It's kind of like the old joke: A man goes to the doctor and says, "It hurts when I do this." The doctor replies, "Then don't do that." At some point, you have to realize your behavior is hurting you and it's time to stop it. Sadly, many don't stop their behavior but continue living with the results of their stupidity.

Some people won't take the steps to learn what it takes to change their lives. They have to be shown a better way. They have to be told exactly what to do. Many are not self-starters. They need someone else to look at their life, tell them it's stupid to be doing what they are doing and then hand them a list of what they should change. For those people, it's a good thing I showed up, because that is what I am doing in this book.

Are there things you would like to know or that you really need to know that you don't know? Is there information that could help you be more successful, healthier, richer and happier, or a better parent? The answer to all of these questions is a resounding "yes." So what are these things?

I warned you that this was coming: Get ready to write them down now. Yes, right now. Don't say to yourself, "I'll wait until later" or "I'll come back to this part." You won't do it. I know you as well as you know yourself. Don't put it off. Just do it. Prove to yourself you are ready to change, and get your pencil and go to work.

MY "I'M IGNORANT ABOUT" LIST:

_____

_____

_____

_____

_____

_____

_____

_____

_____

Did you fill out the list? If you didn't, then you can count this as one more time when you say what you want but aren't willing to do what it takes to get what you want. You have just proved once again that you are no more than a casual observer of success. You aren't seriously committed to becoming more successful. You talk a good game, but you don't deliver. Shame on you.

However, if you did fill out the list, you are a serious student of success with a commitment to changing your results.

PEOPLE ARE STUPID.

I sometimes cover the reasons people aren't successful in my speeches and seminars and then ask, "Now, how many people are really stupid?" Once a guy about three rows from the front raised his hand in response to the question. I stopped and said, "Yeah, I guess you really are." Of course the whole audience laughed. I then stopped and complimented him for being honest, because I don't know anyone who isn't stupid from time to time.

By the way, I know the word *stupid* is offensive to some people. But what else do you call it when someone knows exactly what to do to have a better life, yet won't do it? I think the word *stupid* is perfect for that situation.

Everyone knows what it takes to be successful in most areas. How could you not? Let me prove it:

Want to lose weight? Exercise more, eat less. Simple. Factual. Every doctor knows it. I know it. You know it. You don't need a book, seminar, mentor, coach or television show to tell you that. You know it all on your own.

Want to have more money? Spend less, earn more. Again, no one can argue with that solution. You know this one, too.

Want better kids? Spend more time with them teaching them right from wrong. Duh!

Want a better relationship with your spouse? Talk with each other, spend more time together and care about each other's feelings, emotions and ideas. Come on. Is this stuff hard? No. You know this!

Want to be smarter? Read a book. Take a class. Go to a lecture.

Are these things *all* it takes to lose weight, have more money, have better kids, have better relationships and be smarter? Of course not. It takes more than that, sometimes much more than that, but it's a start. If you did only these few things, you would see a change in your results.

I contend that every person knows exactly what he or she should be doing in every situation for things to be better. You may not know *all* you need to do, but you know *something* you could do. But while people always know something they could do, they rarely do it. That's the really stupid part. That's the part that ticks me off the most. You know what to do and yet you aren't doing it? What kind of person are you?

Okay, it's time for the next list. What do you know you could be doing to improve things that you aren't doing anything about? You have the knowledge, but you are being stupid by not using it. No lecture on the importance of filling out the list this time. You know the drill. Get your pencil and get after it.

MY "I'M STUPID" LIST:

_____
_____
_____
_____
_____
_____
_____
_____
_____
_____

> "Some scientists claim that hydrogen, because it is so plentiful, is the basic building block of the universe. I dispute that. I say there is more stupidity than hydrogen, and that is the basic building block of the universe."
>
> Frank Zappa

PEOPLE ARE LAZY.

Hopefully, I have proven by now that you already know what it takes to be successful. You know what it takes to do better in most, if not all, areas of life. I know you know enough to do better, and you know that you know enough to be doing better. So why aren't you doing better? Got an answer for that one? What's the answer? Or are you stumped? Let me help you with the answer. Like most answers, it is very simple: You are lazy.

You are too lazy to do the things you know you should be

doing to have a better life. What's up with that? How can you look at yourself in the mirror and know that you know how to improve, but are more interested in watching television than being successful?

You could read a book to be more successful, but that rerun of *Seinfeld* you have already seen three times sounds like a better idea to you. Are you kidding me?

You have kids who need help preparing for a spelling test tomorrow but *Monday Night Football* is on and you can't miss that! What a lazy, pitiful parent you are. You have no time for your own kids, but you can find plenty of time to watch a nanny on television raise some other idiot's kids.

You are forty pounds overweight and you know that going for a walk would help you lose weight and live longer, but you are too lazy to do it. Your excuse is that you don't have time for a walk. However, you still have time to watch people lose weight on television on *The Biggest Loser* or *Celebrity Fit Club*.

You hate your job or maybe you don't even have a job, yet you can't find the time to work on your résumé or search the want ads to improve your situation. I bet you didn't miss the latest episode of *The Apprentice*. Can you spell *irony*? Probably not.

You have time to do what feels good. You have time to do what's easy to do. You have plenty of time to do all the things that don't matter at all. You just don't have time to do the important things!

What are the most important things?

Funny how some things seem so important to us when we are doing them. Then when we look back, we realize they weren't so important at all. You know the feeling. It's like finding out you are really good at doing something that doesn't need to be done.

What could possibly be more important to you than living up to your fullest potential? Living as prosperously as you can? Being as healthy as you can? Enjoying your friends and family? Being a good parent? Or spouse? Don't even bother to answer, because if you can come up with anything, it will only prove further what an idiot you are. There is no answer to these questions. Nothing is more important. Period.

I can just see the letters I am going to get because of what I just said. "Haven't you ever heard of being busy, Larry?"

"Easy for you to say that the rest of us are lazy; you are a rich guy writing books. I work two jobs; I am hardly lazy! Where is the time supposed to come from to work on all of these things?"

Okay. You are busy. I get it. And I don't care how busy you are, because it doesn't matter. Is that the epitaph you want on your tombstone? HE WAS TOO BUSY. I want mine to read EMPTY. ALL USED UP. Do you want your dying regret to be "I was too busy to spend time on the important things"? Or do you want to die knowing you did your best in every area of your life and your only regret is that there wasn't time to do even more?

I know people who are extremely busy and still find a way to carve out a little time to work on making their lives better. There are single mothers who work two jobs, take good care of their kids and then go to night school so they will be able to provide a better life for themselves and their kids. How do they do it? I have no idea. They are amazing human beings for sure. But they are no more amazing than you are. Remember, if one can do it, another can do it. The people who figure out how to do it are able to do so because they don't make excuses. They don't give themselves an out. They have no time either, yet a better life matters enough to them to do whatever it takes, whether it is convenient or not.

So I understand you are busy. Just don't let it get in the way of a better life.

If one can do it, another can do it.

I get letters from people just like those single mothers, telling me what they did to become successful. I get them from all kinds of people from all walks of life and ethnic origins, with physical issues, money issues, family issues, really ugly personal histories and more. People tell me what they have overcome to achieve amazing things. Those letters encourage me to keep kicking ass and telling people to get over themselves. Those folks had reasons to be anything but successful, but they got over themselves, got past their excuses and took control of their lives. They were busy, too, but they got it done.

Again, if one can, another can. But not until you admit that you are lazy. I am lazy, too. I admit it. I could do more. You could do more. All I am asking is, what more could you be doing to make your life better?

There are areas of your life where you know you are being lazy. Make the list:

MY "I'VE BEEN LAZY ABOUT" LIST:

_____
_____
_____
_____
_____
_____
_____
_____
_____
_____

PEOPLE DON'T GIVE A DAMN.

If you made it through the first three of my ten ways you are sabotaging your success, being ignorant, stupid and lazy, then you realize there are some things you don't know that you need to know. You are also aware there are things you do know that you aren't doing anything with. If you know what you should be doing and aren't doing it, then it means you are lazy. Why are you lazy? You know it isn't because there isn't enough time. I already covered that. The average millionaire has the same number of hours in his day as the average homeless guy. So what could it be? Hmmm, how about this? You just don't give a damn! Yep, you don't care enough to change. It isn't important to you.

Again, I know I'll take some heat over this one. In fact, when I covered my "stupid, lazy and don't give a damn" philosophy briefly in an earlier book, a woman wrote this review about it:

> *"They don't give a damn." His theory: "if you really cared, you would do what it took to be the best for your spouse" doesn't sit well with me when he trashes the fact that just because you work all day, come home and fix dinner, do dishes, help the kids with homework and baths and maybe squeeze in a little laundry or cleaning well that is just an excuse for "not really taking care of yourself." Um Hello!! I think I would rather be putting on my makeup and fixing my hair "so I can show my spouse how much I care" rather than taking care of the home and family, but Oh Yeah . . . that would make me lazy??*

She's right about me. I do think that if you really gave a damn about your marriage or your husband that from time to time you would let the laundry go, put the kids to bed a little early and fix your hair, put on your makeup and show your spouse how much you care. I believe if more wives did that from time to time, there would be more happy husbands with happier wives and better marriages. I believe the exact same thing applies to men as well. I don't care how tired you are or how hard you have worked or what needs to be done at home, guys. Sometimes, you need to come home, take a shower, spray on a little cologne, put on your nice clothes, hire a babysitter and take your wife someplace really nice for dinner. I believe that you have to care enough to suck it up and do whatever it takes to make a better marriage or a better life or to be a better parent because it's important to you. Is the other stuff important? Of course it is. Sometimes, not every night, but sometimes, you still have to do more.

It is her last question that requires some attention and it is what I am really talking about here: "that would make me lazy??" Maybe it would, but probably not. This woman is clearly doing a lot. I'll give her that, so she isn't lazy. She is doing what is important to her. I just want her to determine what really is important—to go beyond the details and look at the bigger picture. You do what you do because it is important for you to do it. Not because it's convenient or easy or even fun, but because it is important.

It comes down to priorities and balance. Sometimes, the housework must come first. Sometimes, the kids' homework comes first. Sometimes, it's the laundry. However, sometimes you do what it takes regardless of whether you feel like it, want to do it or have the time to do it because the right thing to do is to put your spouse and your relationship first. Everything that is really important requires your attention—sometimes all of your attention. In this woman's case, it's not that the kids or laundry or dinner are more important than her husband, it's just that she has to decide what is most important at any given time and spread her busy life a little thinner to make sure that everything that deserves attention gets attention.

How to figure out what you give a damn about

Life is all about figuring out what is important to you. In *You're Broke Because You Want to Be: How to Stop Getting By and Start Getting Ahead*, I wrote that the way you spend your money shows what is important to you. If looking cute is important to you, then your money will be spent at the mall. If having a financially secure future is important to you, then your money will be saved and invested. See how simple it is? Let me take it a step further. If all your money is spent at the mall, then you don't give a damn about saving your money. In other words, a financially secure future doesn't matter to you because you aren't spending your money in a way that would prove it.

Let's extend that concept beyond money. If you smoke, then you don't give a damn about living a long, healthy life. How could you? You know that the cigarette is going to end your life sooner than it has to end and will dramatically affect your quality of life. Yet you don't give a damn about that. The cigarette is what you really give a damn about. You care more about those moments of self-satisfaction than you care about your health or your family.

If you aren't reading, studying and trying to learn more about being successful, then you don't give a damn about being successful.

If you eat like a pig and end up looking like a pig because of it, then you don't care about your health or about looking good. You also don't give a damn about your family, or you wouldn't be consciously choosing to die earlier than you have to.

Ouch! See how it works? You aren't used to having someone talk to you like this, are you? Some of you are sputtering now about how unfair I am to be making these statements. What is so unfair about any of these statements? Isn't it fair to say that when you put your time, energy and money into an area of your life, that area is important to you? That seems like a perfectly fair statement to me. And if you don't put any time, energy or money into an area of your life, it is because you don't give a damn about that area of your life.

Let's kick it up a notch.

Since the average parent spends only three and a half minutes per week in meaningful conversation with their kids, it must mean that the average parent doesn't give a damn about their kids.

If you smoke, knowing you will die sooner than if you didn't smoke, then you must not give a damn about living.

If you choose to watch television instead of reading a book that might help you get a better job, then you don't give a damn about providing for your family.

If you don't make the effort to give your job your very best while you are there, then you don't give a damn about your job.

If you don't pay your bills on time, then you don't give a damn about keeping your word, and you lack integrity.

If you don't vote in the next election, then you don't give a damn about the direction our country is going in.

If you don't take the time to tell your spouse you love him or show your spouse you love her, or make the effort to let them know you give a damn about them in any way, then it must hold true that you don't give a damn about them.

If you are like the average fifty-year-old in America with less than $2,500 saved, it means you don't give a damn about retirement, or sending your kids to college.

"It's not that black-and-white, Larry."

Oh, yes, it is. Stop buying that crap about life not being black or white. Things are either right or wrong, good or bad, black or white. Stop rationalizing your stupid behavior by putting it in that gray area. When confronted with an answer they don't want to give, people always want to say, "That's a gray area." There is no gray area. Begin to think more in absolutes about getting your life in order and you will find life is much easier. Decisions will also be much easier to make when you think in terms of absolutes. Your excuses won't hold water either, which will move you toward success much faster.

Wait, you say you do give a damn?

Bull. You don't give a damn because you aren't putting any time, energy or money into it.

> *If you aren't putting your time, energy and money into something, then you don't give a damn about it. Your time, energy and money ALWAYS go to what is important to you.*

"But being healthy, having a secure financial future, living a long life . . . all of those things *are* important to me!"

Okay, they are. You win. You have worn me down and I'll stop arguing with you. As of right now, I believe you. Those things are important to you. Your family, your health and the rest are important to you, just not important *enough* to put your time, energy and money into them.

It all comes down to, "Are they important *enough*?"

When do things become important enough to change your behavior?

When it is either too late or almost too late.

Funny how eating healthy foods and exercising aren't important at all *until* you have a heart attack. Then they become your biggest priority. Why did you have to have the heart attack for it to become important? Wouldn't it have been cheaper and less painful *not* to have had the heart attack?

Smoking wasn't a big deal until you got lung cancer. Now you are covered in patches, going to hypnotists and chewing nicotine gum. You couldn't have done all that before you got cancer?

Why do you have to lose your house to finally understand that you have been spending too much at the mall?

Having sex with your spouse wasn't all that important until you found out he was having an affair, was it? Calm down, it works both ways on this one!

Why do you need to lose your family to understand that you should have been spending more time at home and less time at the office?

It's imperative that you determine what is important to you before a tragedy happens. That way you can begin to spend your time, energy and money on the things that matter.

New shoes don't matter in the long run, especially if you are in debt or are behind on your car payment.

That golf game you think you have to play with your buddies isn't nearly as important as time well spent with your wife or kids.

Do you have to give up the shoes and the golf game completely? No. It's about balance. It's about setting priorities. It's about knowing what is really important, and then giving what is really important the proper amount of focus.

The issue is that people don't know what is really important to them. They say they do, but their actions contradict their words. What things do you really give a damn about? Write them down here.

THE THINGS I CARE ABOUT:

You should have written down things like the names of your kids and your spouse. Your health should be on the list. Retirement, college savings, investments and other money issues should have made the list. Helping others with your time and money would have been a nice thing to have on the list as well. The point is to write down things that are really important to you.

Okay, with that list completed, it's time for the next list. This list will show you what you really give a damn about right now, based on the evidence. Forget what you say is important; let's find out what is really important. All you have to do is look at how you are spending your time, energy and money right this minute to fill up this list. I could spend five minutes walking through your house and tell you what is important to you. Give me thirty seconds in your closet or ten minutes with your credit card statement and your bank statement. Show me your calendar. Let me see your checkbook. Spend ten minutes with me, telling me how you spent your free time this week. That's all it takes for me to know what you give a damn about.

Since I am not going to walk through your house or look at your credit card statement or have a conversation with you to find this stuff out, you need to do it for yourself. Spend a few minutes analyzing your life by tracking your actions to figure out what you really care about. Walk through your house with a notepad, writing down what you have on your shelves and in your closet. Look at your checkbook, bank statement and credit card statements to see how you are spending your money. Go look in your garage.

I could also follow you around for one day and find out what you care about based on how you spend your time. I would see how hard you work, how much television you watch, and how much time you spend with your family. I'm obviously not going to be able to follow you around either. So do it yourself. Analyze how you are spending your time and figure out what's important to you.

To do this, I am going to give you another list to complete. This list is going to be based on evidence. Fill out this one after you take a long, hard look at your life. How many hours do you spend with your children? How much time do you spend one-on-one with your spouse? Do you have more DVDs than books? Is your refrigerator full of soda or juice? Frozen pizza or meat and vegetables? Is your closet full and your bank account empty? The answers to those questions will tell you what is really important to you and what you really care about.

Don't cheat when you fill out this list. Don't try to make yourself look better than you do. Be honest. This is not the time for you to fudge the results. This is the time for you to finally come clean with yourself and figure out what is wrong with your life and what you can do to fix it.

THE THINGS I REALLY CARE ABOUT, BASED ON THE EVIDENCE:

Were you honest? Go back through the list quickly right now. Did you leave anything out? As you go through the rest of the book, you will think of other things that should go on this list. When that happens, come back to the list and write down some more of those things.

PEOPLE LACK VISION.

One of the reasons people aren't successful is that they can't create a picture of what success should look like in their lives. They can see success happening in other people's lives, but they can't imagine success happening in their own lives.

They are stuck in a rut, seeing life the way it is or the way it has been instead of the way it could be. You have to move beyond that vision of the way your life has always looked and begin to picture your life the way you want it to look.

Vision in my own life

Based on my background and the way I grew up, I could easily have started out with a vision that was much different from the way my life has turned out to be. I could have held the vision that life would be hard and that I was going to have a hard time keeping up with my bills and would have to struggle to get ahead. I would work hard and have some happy times, but life would be hard at every turn. Since that was the way my parents had lived, that easily could have become reality for me if that had been my vision for my life.

Or I could have gone to work for a big company and had a nice little house on a nice little street in a nice little town in Oklahoma, where I grew up. If that had been my vision, I would still have accomplished more than many others in my family had managed.

However, that was not the way I saw my life unfolding. I have always had a grand vision for my life. When I was thirteen, I decided I wouldn't be broke. I saw myself as being a rich guy someday. I didn't know how I was going to do it, but I held that vision for myself.

Though I came from little and lived in an old World War I barracks that my dad had converted into a house, I saw myself eventually living in a huge house that everyone would walk into and say, "Wow!" I saw myself having closets full of cool clothes and lots of watches and jewelry, living like a millionaire.

When I started in the business of professional speaking, I saw myself as being a huge success. I saw myself as the featured presenter at big corporate events and at huge public events with thousands of people. I was even bold enough to see myself on television.

When I started writing books, I saw myself at the top of the *New York Times* and *Wall Street Journal* bestseller lists.

I was able to picture all of that in my mind. I held that vision of myself even though I had no clue how it was going to happen or when it was going to happen.

Know what? Every one of those things ended up happening and much more. I now get to live the life I pictured.

How did it all happen for me? I held the vision in my mind and then worked hard to make the vision come true. I refused to accept a lesser vision or to ever compromise. Without the vision, I could not have experienced the reality.

You aren't stuck with your current vision.

That's the good news: You can change your vision. You can work to erase the picture you have in your mind and create a new picture. All it takes is some imagination and then some hard work to make what you imagined become your reality.

PEOPLE HAVE LOW EXPECTATIONS.

Most of us have reached the point where we don't expect much from other people. Some of us have become so jaded by bad experiences that we don't expect people to be anything but stupid. I am certainly guilty of this. I start out with the basic premise that people are idiots, and then I wait for them to prove me wrong. The sad thing is that they rarely prove me wrong.

In business, most of us have had so many negative experiences that we are conditioned to expect bad service. Good service comes as a complete and total surprise.

We expect people to be late—to be rude—to do a half-assed job. Why? Because most people are late, rude and do a half-assed job.

We don't expect much from our employees, and they don't disappoint us.

As employees, we don't expect much from our employers, and they are there proving us right at every turn.

We expect teenagers to be rude, uninterested and bored. That's what they give us back: just what we expect from them.

When you don't expect much from people, they don't deliver much. But when you raise your expectations of people, they tend to deliver much more.

> *People will either live up to or down to your expectations of them.*

The solution is to expect more from others.

"But, Larry, aren't you setting yourself up for disappointment this way?"

You bet I am. The bulk of society won't live up to my expectations of them, regardless of what I say or do. You will find that to be true as well. But sometimes, people will surprise you. On the rare occasion when it happens to me—woo hoo!!

Occasionally, you will find that rare individual or company that either meets or even exceeds your expectations. When that happens to me, my faith in humanity is restored. Besides, I find it is better to be disappointed by expecting a lot and getting nothing than by expecting nothing and getting it.

> *It is better to be disappointed*
> *by expecting a lot and getting nothing*
> *than by expecting nothing and getting it.*

I recently decided to add a new entry to my house. Rose Mary and I wanted to put in a Saltillo tile walkway from the driveway to the front door. I talked to the tile company, who said they had a guy they really liked and would do a good job. I called him to set up an appointment. He agreed to a time and, believe it or not, he actually showed up. He took his measurements and said he would fax over a bid later that day. Two days later, I still didn't have a bid. When I called him, he had all kinds of excuses. I told him I expected him to keep his word and counted on people to do what they said they would do when they said they would do it. He apologized and said I would have the bid the next day. I never heard from him again.

I called another guy: Willie of Classic Home Improvements. Willie also showed up on time just like the first guy. I told him of my bad experience with the other guy and that I expect people to do what they said they will do, when they said they would do it, the way they said they would do it. He said that he totally agreed with me and that this would never be an issue with him. I thought to myself, "Yeah, right." He told me that I would have a bid the next day. Sure enough, the next day I had a bid. He called to make sure I had gotten it. He asked what questions I had. He gave me a start date and a completion date, and I asked him if he really meant it. He said, "When I give my word, I mean it. I won't tell you something unless I intend to do it." I hired him. That was one of my best decisions ever. He did my walkway just like I wanted it, on time and for exactly what he said it would cost. There was a never a surprise. I had absolutely nothing to complain about, which is kind of a shame because when it comes to complaining, I am a pro. Because he performed so well, he has now completed a room addition for me, built a retaining wall around my house, covered my bedroom patio and built a wine room, and who knows where it will end? This guy met and then exceeded all my expectations, and I will continue to do business with him because of it.

You also have to expect more from yourself.

It's fairly easy to expect a lot from others. You just draw a line in the sand and decide that you won't compromise your standards. You then communicate those standards to the people you are doing business with and stand behind your word. Not hard at all.

It's amazing how tough it gets when you have to turn the tables and expect more from yourself. That's when you know how serious you are about self-improvement. When you are willing to draw that line in the sand right in front of yourself and not compromise your standards when it comes to your own performance, then you know you are ready to put on your big-boy pants and improve your life. You also might find yourself saying, "Damn, did I have to draw the line so deep?"

When I have high expectations of myself, I feel more personal pride in what I get done. I have higher self-esteem. I impose what some people might call unrealistic expectations on myself—but I also find that I get paid better for my work.

I have raised a family of high achievers because I clearly laid out high expectations for them to live up to. I always expected the best from my sons. I wasn't one of those fanatic dads who screams and yells and belittles his kids into working harder. You know the kind of dad I'm talking about. Go to any Little League game or soccer match and watch those used-to-be, wannabe, never-been jocks embarrassing their kids by jumping up and down on the sidelines, screaming at the players and the coaches and making total asses of themselves. That was never my style. I let the boys pick what they wanted to do based on their interests and then expected them to give it their best shot according to their talents and abilities. If they weren't the best, it didn't mean they shouldn't give it their best. That is all I expected; set a high standard for yourself based on your own best effort and then work hard to do your personal best.

My boys have always seen how hard I was willing to work to be at the top of my game. They saw I expected a lot from myself and was willing to work as hard as I needed to make that happen. They became the same kind of men.

Patrick Winget

My younger son, Patrick, is a fashion designer. He and his buddy Brad Day, who can sell just about anything to anybody, started their own clothing line while Patrick was still in school at the Fashion Institute of Design and Merchandising in Los Angeles. They struggled like all new companies do. They were rich in ideas but had little capital to finance their ideas. However, they made it work. How? Hard work and a willingness to do whatever it took to succeed. Both of them lived on practically nothing. They worked twenty hours a day and spent lots of nights sleeping on the floor of their cramped, trashy little office/manufacturing space. When he did get some money, Patrick spent it on his education. When the choice was between groceries or a book about fashion that would inspire him to create better designs, he would always choose the book. You can skip a meal, but you can't skip a chance for more education and inspiration. Patrick and Brad's little company eventually grew to the point where it either needed a major influx of cash or needed to go away. With no one willing to put the kind of money they needed into it, they had to fold the company. They had a huge bank loan to pay off and they owed me a sizable chunk of change, but they assured me they would make good on both.

Around that time, a customer who had always admired their clothing line put up the money and hired Patrick and Brad to start another line. They are now once again doing what they do best and making a ton of money doing it. They still work long hours and are still willing to do whatever it takes to be success-ful. In three months, they paid off their bank loan. They make regular payments to me and will soon be at zero with the Bank of Larry.

They have both told me many times that they will never be broke again because they expect to be rich and are willing to sacrifice to stay that way. How did they go from broke and struggling to doing so well? Because that's what they expected from themselves.

Tyler Winget

My older son, Tyler, is a cop. He is a really good cop. He is better than he even has to be. He could coast along and not do much except go to work, hand out traffic tickets and draw his paycheck like many of his coworkers. There are a lot of cops who retire having done that. There may not be anything wrong with it if that is your choice, but it isn't the kind of cop Tyler wants to be. He is an adrenaline junky. He craves excite-ment. When he joined the army and had to pick what he wanted to do as his job, the recruiter talked to him about desk jobs and places where he could learn a trade he could use later in civilian life. Tyler responded with, "I want to carry a gun and blow things up." So he became a paratrooper, shot a .50 caliber and became a rifle expert and sniper. As a cop, he likes to fight real crime. He likes blood and battles and putting real bad guys behind bars. You can't be that kind of cop and survive for very long if you aren't willing to be the best at every aspect of your job. Therefore, he will never be the kind of cop who can coast along at anything. He expects too much from himself to coast. He attends every rifle school that is held by the police department. He attends all the training offered from any source available, and he does it at his own expense. He goes to the gym every day so he will be as physically fit as he can be. He goes to Muay Thai kickboxing and Brazilian jiujitsu and boxing and other hand-to-hand combat training because he might need the training someday to save his life or someone else's life. Plus, he likes to hit and be hit. (I don't get that at all, but it's who he is!) Not only does he do those things, but he works hard at every aspect of his job so he can be the best at anything he undertakes. He doesn't have to, I don't expect him to, his wife doesn't expect him to, his job doesn't expect him to, but he expects it from himself. That's what I respect the most: his ability to expect the best from himself and make it happen.

Be proud of yourself.

I am extremely proud of my boys. I am also proud that I was the kind of father who figured out how to instill good qualities in them. However, what matters most is that they are proud of themselves.

The three of us have made the decision to live our lives based on excellence. Why? Because we can. Again, it's not about being *the* best—it's about doing *our* best.

What do you expect from yourself? You know my take would be that you are getting exactly what you expect from yourself. That ugly little point keeps popping up, doesn't it?

You are living the life you expect to live. If you expected more, you would be getting more.

You know the next step. Make a list of what you expect from yourself.

WHAT I EXPECT FROM MYSELF:

_____

_____

_____

_____

_____

_____

_____

_____

_____

_____

_____

As you filled out that list, did you think about whether you are expecting the best from yourself? If you didn't, go back and check your list to make sure you are expecting your very best.

PEOPLE DON'T RECOGNIZE THE CONSEQUENCES OF THEIR ACTIONS.

The single most popular question I get as I do interviews on the radio, on television or for magazines or newspapers is this: Why do people do the stupid things they do? It doesn't matter whether I am talking about business, money, parenting, relationships or any other area of life.

It is such an easy answer: People do what they do because they believe there are no consequences for doing otherwise.

> *People are the way they are because they believe there are no consequences for being otherwise.*

Remember the old joke, "Why does a dog lick himself?" Answer: "Because he can." Why do people do what they do? Because they can.

For the most part, people will get by with whatever they can if there are no consequences. Consequences control behavior. Bad behavior with a lack of consequences will be repeated.

Consequences control behavior.

I spoke of this concept in regard to managing employees in my book *It's Called Work for a Reason! Your Success Is Your Own Damn Fault.* When dealing with employees, if you want to see them repeat any good behavior, all you have to do is reward that behavior. Good behavior when rewarded will be repeated. This concept works just as well when you turn it around. Bad behavior when ignored will be repeated. Ignoring the behavior *is* the reward.

If your kid throws a ball in the living room and breaks a lamp and nothing happens, the chances are very good that your kid will continue to throw the ball in the living room.

If a company delivers bad service, yet people continue to spend their money with that company, then there are no consequences for the company and the bad service will continue.

If an employee comes in fifteen minutes late and no one

says anything, then chances are she will do it again. Why shouldn't she? If there are no consequences, then the behavior will continue until the behavior becomes a habit. Behavior that has gone to the point of becoming a habit is very difficult to break. Better to catch it when it happens the first time instead of waiting until a habit has formed. (More on breaking bad habits is coming up soon.)

If I tell you that if you touch the top of a stove you will get burned, and then you touch it and get burned, chances are you won't touch the stove again. If you do and get burned a second time, you really are an idiot! The pain from getting burned is the consequence, and it will probably keep the second time from happening. You will have learned your lesson.

I am a big believer in enforcing consequences and letting people experience the pain of their bad decisions. Only then can the lesson be learned.

Stupidity should create pain!

On my television show *Big Spender* on A&E, where I coached people in debt, I always liked it when I confronted people with their situation and they cried. I loved those tears! Is it because I'm mean? No, it's because when someone experiences the pain of their stupidity, they are more likely to change their behavior.

That is the reason I am so opposed to government bailouts. First of all, any time the government gets involved, it always ends up taking longer than promised, it is more complicated than it should be and costs are more than expected. Mostly I am against government bailouts because the people who get bailed out won't experience the pain of their mistakes.

When people buy a house they can't afford, then default on the loan, the bank will foreclose on them. Those are the rules. It was clearly laid out in the contract when they bought the house, so it should come as no surprise. If the government bails them out and in essence they get by with their mistake, the people will not have experienced the pain of their behavior, meaning there will have been no consequences. And there will have been no lesson learned.

About half the people who file for bankruptcy end up filing bankruptcy again. The first bailout didn't teach them any lesson. Since no lesson was learned, the behavior that got them in trouble the first time is repeated.

Life's penalty box

The reason that limits, contracts, codes, laws, rules, even fences exist is to establish ethical, moral and physical boundaries for society to live by in order to coexist in a peaceful, reasonable manner. When you cross the line and break the rules, there have to be consequences; otherwise, we would have chaos.

Games have rules. If you break the rules, you experience the consequences. Can you imagine something as simple as a game of checkers where there were no rules? People screaming "KING ME!" just because they showed up? That's not right! Even hockey, a game where you can get in a fistfight, knock a guy's teeth out and still keep playing, has some rules and consequences. Hockey has a penalty box, that special little place you go when you break the rules.

Life has a penalty box, too. Of course it isn't called a penalty box, because sadly we don't consider our results to be penalties.

In life, the penalty box is called sickness, unemployment, poverty, unhappiness and loneliness. You probably never thought about those things as penalties, but they are. Each of those situations is a consequence. They are the consequences of your decisions, ideas, beliefs, thoughts, words and actions.

Most people don't seem to be able to see the correlation between their behavior and their results. Instead they either call it bad luck or want to lay blame on society. We all are experiencing the consequences of our choices; while painful, those consequences are our lessons. Learn the lessons and you can have whatever you are willing to work for. Ignore the lessons and you will be doomed to repeat the lesson until you do learn it. You will stay locked in the penalty box forever.

Years ago, I made some stupid decisions in my telecommunications business. Those decisions resulted in my business going bankrupt. Because I was the company president and it was my signature on all those loan documents and tax preparations, I ended up going bankrupt, too. It was tough on me. It was humiliating, embarrassing and financially devastating. However, it was the best thing that ever happened to me. That experience, brought about by my actions and decisions, taught me valuable lessons about life, business and money. Those lessons are the things I now teach to earn my living. Those lessons are the reason you are reading this book. I could have become bitter and whined and wallowed in my misery. I could have stayed broke and gone on food stamps. I could have said, "I'm never going to run another business!" and then taken a job working for someone else. I didn't do any of those things. I sucked it up and started again. I'm not bragging. There was nothing all that special about what I did. People have overcome much bigger obstacles than I have to become more successful than I am. I tell you the story to prove that life offers lessons. The lessons are delivered in the form of consequences. I had mine. It wasn't pleasant. In fact, luckily, it was so unpleasant that I refused to experience it again. Therefore, I did all I could to learn my lesson and not repeat it. The result for me was success.

> *"If the people who make the decisions are the people who will also bear the consequences of those decisions, perhaps better decisions will result."*
>
> John Abrams, *The Company We Keep*

MY "CONSEQUENCES" LIST:

> *"In nature, there are neither rewards nor punishments—there are consequences."*
> Robert G. Ingersoll

PEOPLE HAVE BAD HABITS.

This is where we are: People do stupid things. Because they don't recognize the consequences of doing those stupid things, people keep doing them. Those things become acceptable and get repeated over and over again until they become habits. It is a simple process that gets repeated in a million different ways every day. The first time you ever put on socks, you might have started with your left foot. You started with your left foot first again the second time you put on your socks. After a few weeks of putting on your socks left foot first, it became your habit. Now if you tried to put your socks on by beginning with your right foot, it would feel very foreign to you. That's the way habits work. We don't recognize that they are habits until they are already formed and deeply ingrained. By then, it's too late. We've got them whether we ever wanted them or not. Putting on socks is no big deal. It doesn't really matter how you do it or which foot you start with. Putting on your socks is totally insignificant. Other things aren't that insignificant. Some things *do* matter. Most habits have a bigger impact on your life and the lives of those around you than putting on your socks.

Bad habits

Most people think they know what their bad habits are. I have talked with people about having bad habits, and many respond with something like, "I don't have any bad habits: I don't drink or smoke." Some people think those are the only bad habits that count. Bad habits do tend to get categorized as things like smoking, eating too much, spending too much and other things that have well-publicized negative effects. However, some of the most damaging bad habits are subtler than that. Bad habits don't always have visible, immediate negative effects, but over the course of a lifetime they can kill your chances for success.

For instance, I have a few friends who are habitually late. They know what time they agreed to be there and yet can never seem to get there on time. Showing up late is disrespectful to the people you agreed to meet. Carry that over to dealing with customers and you can lose customers. That habit is one that can easily be remedied. Start earlier. Realize that you have given your word and you are a person who keeps his or her word. Being late is a simple example with profound negative effects. There are many bad habits that are even subtler that many people don't think about.

Bad grammar is a bad habit that can kill your chances for success. So is dressing like a slob. Or having an affected way of speaking, like some of the young ladies out there who talk like Valley girls. That particular bad habit will cost you because it will affect your ability to be taken seriously. Would you want to hire an attorney who spoke that way? "Like, oh my God, like, uh, can you, like, totally imagine? You know. I mean, really!" No, you want her to have a voice that has authority and to be able to communicate.

Or how about this speaking style: "You know what I'm talking about?" No. I don't know what you're talking about. Or, "That's what *I'm* talking about!" I know—you were just talking about it.

The only way to break a bad habit

Regardless of the kind of habits you form, good or bad, they are always hard to break. Studies tell us that it takes twenty-one days to either make or break a habit. That means, if you want to break a habit, you have to stop doing what you are doing for three weeks. That's tough to do. The key to breaking a bad habit is to replace what you were doing with something else. You can't just stop doing something—you have to replace it with a new activity. If you go to the mall every Saturday morning and end up spending money you don't have, then replace going to the mall with a new activity. Try the library, the park or any other activity that won't tempt you to spend money. Your new habit is to go to that new place on Saturday mornings. Go ahead and go, but go someplace with positive results instead of negative.

Don't rely on your willpower. Willpower is overrated. Let's say your habit is to eat a big dinner and then sit on your butt watching television for three or four hours until you drop off to sleep, then wander into the bedroom and crash until the alarm goes off and you have to go to work. By the way, I have just described the typical evening of about 80 percent of all adults. If that habit has left you fat, stupid and lazy (the result of doing that night after night), then you might want to break that habit. Okay, so how are you going to do it? Just stop? How are you going to stop? Answer me! Exactly—you can't just stop doing something. You have to replace the bad habit with a new habit. What are you going to do instead of leaving the dinner table and parking yourself in front of the television? You have to know; otherwise, you won't be able to break the habit. Willpower will run thin if you don't plan out a replacement activity. If you decide to spend the time reading instead of watching television, I suggest you have some books lined up to read. Otherwise, there will be nothing to fill the time and you will find yourself right back in front of the flat screen. If you choose to spend it playing with your kids, then I suggest you have a game or activity lined up in advance. Have a new activity ready to replace the old activity; otherwise, you will slip right back into the old behavior.

What are your habits? Take a minute and figure out what you do every day that has created the life you are living. Of course, it won't take more than five seconds to come up with the obvious "bad" habits. It will take a little longer to come up with the subtle habits that are destroying your future. This one requires some thought. Go to work.

MY "HABITS" LIST:

_____

_____

_____

_____

_____

_____

_____

_____

_____

_____

_____

_____

_____

_____

_____

_____

_____

_____

_____

The only way to get rid of these bad habits is to replace them with something new. Know in advance what the new thing is going to be. Write down some activities you could do to fill the hole left by the bad habit you are getting rid of.

MY NEW REPLACEMENT ACTIVITIES:

_____

_____

_____

_____

_____

_____

_____

_____

_____

_____

_____

> *"When you sow an action, you reap a habit.*
> *When you sow a habit, you reap a character.*
> *When you sow a character, you reap a destiny."*
>
> **Unknown**

PEOPLE HAVE POOR ROLE MODELS.

I like all things furry and feathered. I grew up on a farm with all sorts of animals and fowl. I also watch a lot of nature shows on television. I have learned a lot about life from watching animals. One of the things I learned is that geese, like many other fowl, imprint. Imprinting is what happens when a gosling (baby goose) is born. Goslings imprint on whatever animal they see when first born and recognize it as their parent. That is why people must not handle orphaned goslings, for the gosling will imprint on the human. Many shows have been done about this topic. There was even a movie called *Fly Away Home* that covered how some geese imprinted on people and then couldn't fly because they didn't have the right role models to show them how. The people ended up having to teach the geese to fly.

People imprint in much the same way geese do. We imprint and mimic what we see as young, impressionable babies. It forms our beliefs about who we are and what we are capable of. You learn the language you speak because that is what you hear every day. You learn your table manners by watching how your family eats. You even learn what to eat because of what your role models eat. You will develop your likes and dislikes because of the things your parents and siblings like and dislike.

It goes much further. If you grow up in a house where your family doesn't work and expects to be taken care of by the government instead of getting a job and working for a living, then you probably won't spend much time working. Instead, you will spend your days watching the mailbox, waiting for your check. That's how we end up with fifth-generation welfare recipients.

If you grow up in a house where people have a work ethic and a sense of integrity and pay their bills on time, then chances are good that you will become that kind of person as well.

My dad never liked football. Never once in all my years of growing up did we ever have a football game on the television. Therefore, I don't give a hoot about football. My dad liked boxing. When I was a little boy, after *The Phil Silvers Show* ended, Gillette's *Friday Night Fights* would come on. We would fix popcorn and watch the fights. Therefore, I am a boxing fan. Amazingly enough, when boxing comes on television, I also get a craving for popcorn. That was my imprinting.

Fat little kids almost always have fat mamas and daddies.

Kids who enjoy reading are from families where reading is important.

Abusive individuals generally grew up in homes where at least one of the parents was abusive.

Kids who like sports come from families where sports are a part of their lives.

We all imprint.

We learn by watching other people: parents, older brothers and sisters, aunts and uncles, teachers and people on television. We all learn to act in a certain way from watching other people act in certain ways.

Your parents taught you what was acceptable behavior and what was unacceptable behavior based on their actions. They became your example and you followed it. You followed it until your experiences, knowledge base and sphere of influence expanded and you learned new ways of acting.

As a parent, you set the example for your children as well. What kind of example are you setting? I could spend a lot of time on this one, but I think I'm going to save that for a book all its own. I am going to call it *Stop Raising Stupid Kids.*

My point is this: Poor role models are one of the reasons that people do stupid things. This is a valid excuse—for a while. As with all things, you have to become aware enough of your life to realize that it's time to grow beyond your role models and step up to a new level of performance based on what you know is the correct behavior.

Paying for a poor role model

Some people even pay poor role models to help them become more successful. Consider life coaches—a profession that for the most part could be known as "the blind leading the blind."

All you have to do is go online and spend $99 for an online

course and you can be a "certified" life coach. Of course, you can spend up to $15,000 and two years to become a life coach, too. There is no nationally recognized standard or accreditation process for life coaches or life-coaching schools, so anyone can pretty much start a school and pass out a certificate and bestow the title on you. It takes more money and more work to become an umpire than it does to become a life coach. And it probably pays better. It probably even helps more people. Plus, when you become an umpire, you get a whistle! I would put more faith in the guy with the whistle than with most life coaches.

I recently got a letter from a woman who told me it was her life dream to be a life coach. She explained that she had a passion for helping other people. Everyone she met told her she was a good listener. So she put those two things together in her mind and decided that becoming a life coach was the perfect answer because those were the keys, in her opinion, to being able to coach people. She begged me to help her realize her dream. She said she could be the "best life coach ever!" if she weren't broke, weren't so afraid of failing, had some support and was in a good relationship. Are you laughing at this point? I know I was as I read her letter. I told her I couldn't help her with her dream. I told her she had nothing to offer except a desire to help others. She had the ability to listen to people whine about their pitiful lives just like she was asking me to do. She *needed* a life coach more than she needed to *become* one. I also wanted to tell her that she needed a basic course in grammar and a spelling lesson more than she needed anything else, but I was feeling benevolent and skipped that part.

"But everyone needs a helping hand sometimes, Larry."

The best helping hand you will ever find is at the end of your own wrist.

My point is this: Don't pay someone else to fix the mess you made. Especially when they are probably a bigger mess than you are.

> *Don't pay someone else*
> *to clean up the mess you made.*

Not all coaching is a bad thing. I am not against being coached through various situations in life. My company even offers coaching on my material for those with a specific goal who need help and encouragement reaching it. Coaching through a specific process or situation is not the same thing as people who rely on coaching to help them with their daily lives. So my comments here are not an indictment of coaching, or of everyone who is a life coach. I am saying make sure you really need coaching before you pay for it. I am also suggesting that you check the credentials of the person doing the coaching. If he or she isn't more successful than you are, that person is wasting your time and has nothing to teach you.

I'm sure there are some great people in the profession who actually help others. However, it is a profession packed with charlatans, so be careful. I'll spin an old saying around to apply to this point: "Those who can't, coach." They also become motivational speakers. In fact, many motivational speakers who weren't able to make a living speaking have become life coaches in order to survive financially. Just the kind of person you want to coach you, right? A broke, unsuccessful person whose best advice is to have a positive attitude about it.

In fairness, I know those statements are generalizations, much like the old expression "The cobbler's children have no shoes." I am sure there are some cobblers whose children have shoes. But these generalizations are meant to serve as a warning: Make sure the people you pay to teach you have something to teach. Make sure they are examples of the way you want to live. Make sure they have done what they are being paid to help you do.

I owned a business once that ended up in deep trouble. I hired a couple of business coaches/consultants to come in and advise me. After paying way too much money and listening to them tell me stuff I already knew, I found out they were in worse shape than I was. They looked good. They sounded good. They were good salesmen. But they were a mess. Their own business was barely scraping by and they were broke. As a result, I became skeptical of all consultants, coaches, advisors, writers and speakers. I want credentials. I want proof. I want a history of results.

When I hire a financial advisor, I want him to make more or at least as much money as I do and to have his own money in what he wants me to invest mine in.

When I hire a doctor, I want him to be an example for me to aspire to.

I want my insurance agent to have more insurance than he wants me to have.

I want my dentist to have better teeth than I do.

I want the person I turn to for business advice to be better at running a business than I am.

Before you shell out your hard-earned dough to someone to have them help you, make sure they are better at it than you are. Ask good questions. Find out the truth.

Not me

Some of you might be thinking that what I do makes me a life coach. Please don't call me that. As Kierkegaard said, "To label me is to diminish me." All I do—repeat—*all I do* is remind you that you have the ability to change your own life. You have the power to do it. You don't need anyone else. You need to recognize your mistakes and remind yourself that you can change when you are ready to do what it takes to change. I only provide the tools. Think of me as the hardware store. I won't build your house, but I'll sell you the tools to do it. It's up to you to take them home and use them.

LESSONS I HAVE LEARNED FROM MY ROLE MODELS:

PEOPLE HAVE NO PLAN.

As I write this, I am watching a television report about Ed McMahon and how he is facing losing his house to foreclosure. Poor old Ed at the age of eighty-five is in financial trouble because he hasn't been able to work for eighteen months because of his health. It seems he broke his neck and hasn't been able to work. Hey, Ed, why do you still have to work at the age of eighty-five? With your career and all the money you have made, your house isn't paid for? Come on! In this interview, Ed said he needed to have had a better plan. You think?

This story is sad. Not because Ed is losing his house; that's his own stupid fault. It's sad because it is proof that regardless of how much money you make and how famous you are, you have to have a plan. I guess Ed did have a plan, but it doesn't seem like it was a very good one, does it? I wonder who sold Ed on that plan?

Everybody is working a plan. You are either working your own plan or someone else's plan. The problem is that, for most people, it isn't a very good plan. How do I know that? I just look at the results. If you don't have good results, then you aren't working a very good plan.

What is your plan?

You are living it right now. How is your plan working for you? Do you have the life you want? Are you as successful as you want to be? Why not? Your plan gave you the results you have.

While people will spend all week planning for their day off, they won't spend one minute planning the rest of their lives. When it comes to that day off, they will decide exactly what they are going to do, who they are going to do it with, how long it is going to take and what it will cost them. Am I right?

Why not do the same things for your life? What work are you going to do, what kind of fun are you going to have, who are you going to do it with and how much is it going to cost? Sound reasonable? Okay, so what is your plan? Don't have one? Sure you do, it just isn't a very good one.

Most people's plan is vague and incomplete. They say stupid stuff like, "I just want to be happy." Not that being happy is stupid, but what is it going to take for that to happen? I just want to be happy, too. But I know that for me that means I need to be healthy, have enough money to do what I want and do something that fulfills me professionally and allows me the time to enjoy my family and friends. What is your plan for being happy? Saying it won't make it happen. Having a plan increases your chances, though, for sure!

I have a list. It's a big list. It's a list for my life in all kinds of areas. There are time frames on some of the things and there are things that don't have a time frame. There are things that revolve around my health, my stuff, my career, my leisure time, my family and some deep dark secret stuff that matters only to me. I have specific plans for some of the items on my list. I know exactly what I have to do to make those things happen. I know I need to read some stuff to increase my knowledge to make some of those things happen. On other stuff, I need to save some money to make them happen. On others, I need to be willing to carve out some time.

At this point, I don't want you to get caught up in the details of exactly how to make your plan happen. I will show you how to do that later. Right now, all I want you to do is write down your plan. What do you want your life to look like? What would you like to do? Where would you like to go? Who do you want to spend your time with? How much money is it all going to take? Got it? Go to work.

MY PLAN FOR MY LIFE:

Financial: _____
_____
_____
_____
_____
_____

Physical: _____
_____
_____
_____
_____
_____

Mental: _____
_____
_____
_____
_____
_____

Social: _____
_____
_____
_____
_____
_____

Career: _____
_____
_____
_____
_____
_____

Spiritual: _____

_____

_____

_____

_____

Family: _____

_____

_____

_____

_____

Other secret stuff: _____

_____

_____

_____

_____

Give it up.

Earlier, I talked about how success is not about getting, but about giving up. Now that you have a plan for what you want, you need a plan for what you are willing to give up.

What are you going to give up to become healthier? Smoking? Fast food?

What are you willing to give up to have more money? Shopping?

What are you willing to give up in order to spend more time with your kids? Golf? Working late?

See how it works? Look back at your plans and write down what you plan to give up.

MY "GIVE UP" LIST:

CHAPTER THREE

HOW DO I STOP BEING AN IDIOT?

Now you have been through the ten ways you are sabotaging your life. I know at least one of them applies to you and your situation. I know this because many of them apply to me. No one is free of self-sabotaging behavior. By now, you should have some clues about what you can do to turn your life around. At this point, the journey has begun and you probably want to know what you can do to live the life you have always dreamed of. Good. Here you go:

To stop being an idiot it takes only three things: recognition, education and application.

RECOGNITION   EDUCATION   APPLICATION

RECOGNITION

The first step is to recognize that you have been messing up. If you don't recognize you have a problem, then you have no hope of fixing it.

This is the first step of every twelve-step program: admitting that you are what you are. So, if you have been an idiot—and we all have—then stop right now and just admit you are an idiot. Have your own little Idiots Anonymous meeting and say,

"Hi, my name is Larry and I'm an idiot." (Only don't be an idiot—use *your* name, not mine.) There is no shame in admitting you have done stupid things in your life. However, there is shame in being an idiot by having everyone else know you are an idiot and then denying you are an idiot. That's just downright embarrassing.

Remember when Star Jones took off for a few weeks when she was on *The View*? (Yes, I watch *The View*. It's one of my indulgences.) Then Star immediately lost about a thousand pounds? It was obvious she had undergone gastric bypass surgery. The entertainment news programs all talked about it and everyone pretty much knew it. But Star denied it—thus proving she was an idiot. She could have admitted it and no one would have cared. In fact, who on the planet really gives a rat's ass about what Star Jones does anyway? It was the denial that proved she was an idiot.

"Mission Accomplished." This was on a banner flying on the deck of a naval ship as George W. Bush stood in front of it and told us we had accomplished our goal after the U.S. attack on Iraq. That has to be one of the most idiotic statements ever made to the American public. I don't know of one human being except George W. Bush who doesn't know what a mistake that statement was. Will he admit it? Nope. The whole world knows—yet he won't come clean and just say that perhaps, *possibly*, **maybe** that was a mistake to claim. George is an easy target for sure, but that statement as much as any of his other blunders proves he is an idiot. Don't write me about this one, folks; it's not about being Republican or Democrat or Libertarian or Independent. It's about saying something stupid and recognizing it was a stupid thing to say, especially when the whole world knows it.

"I did not have sex with that woman." Come on, Billy! You did. I know you were behind the eight ball on this one, but you should have told the truth. It wasn't the sex that got you in trouble. It was the lie. I love him, but at that moment I knew Bill Clinton was being an idiot.

Paris Hilton went to jail for violating her probation. In jail she found God, and the Bible became her favorite book. A few days later, while making an appearance on *Larry King Live*, Larry asked her favorite Bible verse and she couldn't think of even one verse. Guess she forgot. Then again, poor Paris forgets a lot of things—I've seen the pictures.

Jimmy Swaggart—a shining example!

I love Jimmy! This poor guy was a total idiot and yet I completely respect the good old Reverend Swaggart. Why? Jimmy picked up a hooker and got caught. Stupidity of biblical proportion. Or as we say in Oklahoma, "He peed in his chili." Did he deny it? Hell, no! He went before his faithful congregation on national television and admitted his mistake. He cried and begged forgiveness. He said, "I have sinned!" Tears ran down his face and we saw real wailing and gnashing of teeth.

I never thought Jimmy Swaggart could teach me much of anything. But in that moment, Jimmy taught me—and the rest of the world—a great lesson: When you are an idiot, don't make any excuses. Just admit it, and ask forgiveness.

I even created an exercise dedicated to the memory of Jimmy and his television reckoning. I call it the Jimmy Swaggart Moment. In fact, on the *Today* show I told Matt Lauer that people in financial trouble should go to the mirror, look themselves in the eye and have a Jimmy Swaggart Moment.

We have all done things that we should feel bad about. We have said things and done things that have affected others as well as ourselves. The awareness and recognition of your own stupidity is the first step in turning things around.

Have a Jimmy Swaggart Moment of your own. You will be better for it. Look yourself in the eye and admit your stupidity. Let a few tears run down your face. After you have done that, go the extra mile right here and right now and write down your Jimmy Swaggart Moment.

MY JIMMY SWAGGART MOMENT:

_____

_____

_____

_____

_____

_____

_____

_____

_____

Did you do it? Did you have your moment? Now that you've had it, get over it. I know, I beat you up until you finally admitted your mistakes and took responsibility for them. I told you to go to the mirror and shed a tear or two. I even made you write it all down. Now I am telling you to get over it. Listen to me on this one: Don't wallow in your stuff for too long. It becomes annoying to have someone continuously apologizing and reminding us of what an idiot they've been. We know already! So fix it and move on. This idea is the result of something my own son Tyler said to me when he informed me he had figured out the key to success at the age of nineteen. He said it comes down to this:

> _"When you mess up, big deal! Just admit it, fix it and move on."_
>
> Tyler Winget

Good advice, son.

Do it right now. Move on. But where to? What's next?

Recognition of the situation is the first step. Education and application are the next steps.

EDUCATION

> *"The Lord gave you two ends, one for sitting*
> *and one for thinking.*
> *Your success depends upon which one you use.*
> *Heads you win, tails you lose."*
> Tim Hansel

People would *do* better if they simply *knew* better. Education fixes that.

Here is the problem I see with most teaching that goes on: We teach people what the right behavior is before we teach them what the wrong behavior is. When you are working with people who don't know any better (the ignorant referred to earlier), you can begin with teaching the correct behavior. The same applies to kids. You save a lot of time teaching kids the correct way to live, eat and behave from the get-go so they don't have to un-learn that behavior down the line. But when people have spent years doing the wrong thing, there is a considerable amount of unlearning that has to take place before people can begin to learn the correct action to take. That's why my approach is different from that of most of the success gurus. I show you that what you are doing isn't giving you the results you want and then show you the right thing to do. Most teachers do the opposite and teach you the way you should be doing it without proving that you have to unlearn the wrong behavior first.

This happens a lot when it comes to money. Financial gurus are out there trying to teach people how to get rich. There are as many ways to get rich as there are rich people. There is no one single way to get rich. Regardless of which way you choose, you aren't going to get rich until you stop doing the things that are keeping you broke. I recently spoke at a big public rally where the theme was wealth. This "wealth weekend" included various experts going onstage convincing people that you could get rich by selling crap on the Internet and by buying foreclosed homes and by all kinds of various means. "You, too, can be a millionaire—it's quick and it's easy!" was the primary theme. I was the closing speaker. I told them that while it was possible to get rich and become a millionaire by following the various methods described, it was still highly unlikely it would ever happen. Then I asked them, "So if you do all it takes and become rich, what are you going to do with the money? Do you have a plan? Or do you just want the money?" These people wanted to make the money but didn't have a plan for spending it, investing it or using it. They would still have had the habits of a broke person. They would just have become a broke person with money. I don't teach people to get rich; I teach them what it takes to stop being broke. You have to teach people how to stop living like a broke person and start living like a rich person before the money actually shows up. This idea works in every area of life.

You can't teach people how to be healthy until you teach them what they are doing that is unhealthy.

You can't teach people to be good parents until you teach them what they are doing that makes them bad parents.

You can't teach people the right thing to do until you teach them to stop doing the wrong thing. They won't know it is the wrong thing until they see the negative consequences of their behavior. When they become aware of the negative consequences and understand it was their own action that created those consequences, then they will begin to understand what the wrong action is and be more willing to change.

However, education is effective in reaching your goals only when you want to learn. People want to learn most when the stakes are highest.

There was a time when I was a successful small business owner in the telecommunications industry. This story has been told in great detail in my other books and I'm not going to beat that dead horse again here. Many people know that I was successful and then lost it all through a series of bad decisions and stupid mistakes. It is the next part of the story that proves my point about the importance of reading and learning.

After I lost my business, I made the decision that what I really wanted to do was to become a professional speaker. All I had ever really wanted was an audience, and I knew I had something worthwhile to say and was good at saying it. My goal was to be a sales trainer since I had written a lot of sales training material in the past and was an award-winning salesperson and sales manager. When I told my wife that I was going to become a professional speaker, she said, "You don't really know anything about that business, do you?" I had to admit that I didn't. I knew about business and how to run a successful one, and I also knew how to send one into bankruptcy, but I didn't have a clue how the speaking business worked. So I went to work. I started studying the business of professional speaking. I interviewed speakers who were making a lot of money and I interviewed speakers who were struggling and not making any money. I decided to follow the path of those who were making money. (By the way, that is a clue. Always follow the path of people who are making money when you are looking for success in business.)

However, I studied much more than just the business side of speaking. I studied what other speakers were saying. I wanted to know what all the "greats" were talking about—not so I could copy them, but so I could say something different. I also wanted to know how they were saying it and why people were paying them so much money to say it. I became a student of their style. I watched and listened to the great speakers, preachers, politicians and authors. At one time, I owned over 150 audio series and many more videos produced by

Nightingale-Conant. I was probably their best customer at that time. Twenty years later, I have my own successful Nightingale-Conant series entitled *Success Is Your Own Damn Fault!* My goal to have my own educational series with Nightingale-Conant appeared on my goals list for twenty years before I finally got the call.

I listened to every one of those series and watched every video at least twenty times. Not only was I learning about speaking, but I was also getting lots of personal development teaching of my own, which was an added benefit. At the same time, I was reading at least three books per week, developing the best habit I have ever acquired: voracious reading.

Why did I do all of this? The stakes were high. I had just gone bankrupt. I needed the money. I needed a "win." I was desperate to be a success as a speaker. I had no time to be anything but successful. Therefore, I was willing to do whatever it took to become successful.

I remember attending my very first meeting of the Oklahoma Speakers Association. When I introduced myself to many of the more seasoned speakers and told them I was just getting started and was ready to become a huge success, one of the guys laughed and said, "It takes at least five or six years to become any kind of success in this business." I told him I didn't have five or six years. I didn't even have five or six weeks—I had to become successful immediately. With that as your goal, your need and your burning desire, education takes on real meaning to you.

Sure enough, in just five or six weeks, I was able to begin making a pretty good living. Twenty years later, those guys who laughed at me at that meeting are still struggling to make a living.

Are you desperate for some real success in your life? Do you have a burning desire to be happier, more successful and more prosperous? If so, then the time it takes to read a few books, go to a couple of classes, listen to some audios and watch some videos won't seem like much of a sacrifice in your pursuit of a better life.

Education clears up bad information.

Another great thing about getting more education is that it can clear up a lot of the bad information you have learned.

> *"It's not what a man knows that hurts him;*
> *it's what he knows that just ain't so that hurts him."*
> Mark Twain

All of us have learned bad information that is affecting our lives. We have heard it so much and lived by it so long that we would swear that it's true.

My mother always told me, if you don't wear a hat during the winter and your head gets cold, you will catch a cold. Not wearing a hat won't cause you to catch a cold. My mom is not a stupid woman. She taught me a lot about life and how to be a good person and lots of other valuable things. But on this one, she is dead wrong. However, this was one of those things she learned growing up from her mother, and she believes those things to be true. Nothing I say to her is going to change her mind. She learned bad information and never moved past it. That's what she believes, and for her, it has become her reality.

Just a few hundred years ago, people thought the world was flat. The popularly held belief was that you could get in a boat and sail right off the edge of the world. While it wasn't true, it was a limiting belief that inhibited the actions of all the people in the world. It wasn't until a few guys dared to challenge that belief that the world expanded and everything changed.

You have learned certain things and believe them to be true, and the fact is, some of those things are just wrong. Those incorrect beliefs are limiting your success. Education can help you weed out the information you think is right but is in fact wrong. Some information has to be unlearned.

Education alone won't change things for you. Just like the few guys who got in those boats and challenged the thinking of the scholars that the world was flat, you, too, have to take action. You have to get in your own little boat and sail to what you thought was the edge just to prove you can go farther.

The knowledge alone won't expand your world. You have to apply it.

APPLICATION

Damn! It keeps coming back to application, doesn't it? Application is also known as taking action. It's also known as good old-fashioned hard work. You can say you need to apply yourself, and folks will smile and nod with you in agreement. You can say you should take action on what you know, and people will respond with, "Of course." But when you call it work, people cringe. Regardless of what people say, the reality is, they would rather do anything than work.

Of course, we have this new generation of idiots who say that work isn't even work as long as you love what you do. That, folks, is a total load of crap! Any person who tells you that all you have to do is love what you do and it won't seem like work is a complete and utter idiot. I like what I do quite a bit, yet most days, it still feels like work. I even love some of what I do a good bit of the time, yet it's still work. That's okay with me because I understand the truth about work: Work is work! It's not called playtime. It's not called socializing time. It's not called having a good time. It's called work! I even wrote a book entitled *It's Called Work for a Reason!*, which covers this concept and many other aspects of work.

The critical step of taking action, aka going to work, is the one step that gets skipped the most. In fact, there is a whole school of thought that says you don't really need to work because you can think your way to success! Have you been to that school? It's a school for bozos! The graduates of this school end up with a diploma in disappointment. You cannot think your way to success.

> *Wishful thinking is not*
> *a strategy for success.*

You can want to be thinner and hope 24/7 that you will reach your ideal weight, but until you get off your fat butt and take action, you are going to stay fat.

You can have the world's best plan to sell more, but until you start talking to customers, it won't happen.

You can have the best intentions to spend more time with your family, but until you actually start clocking some minutes and hours with them, those intentions are empty words.

Don't tell me what you have planned. Don't waste my time or your own time by filling my ears with your detailed strategy for success. Just show me what you are doing to be successful. Your actions tell me all I need to know. It's great to have a detailed strategic plan, but unless you take action on your plan, they're just words.

If you tell me you are getting up at six A.M. to get in thirty minutes of reading before the rest of your family wakes up, I'll believe you are serious. Notice I didn't say "going to get up at six A.M." I said "getting up at six A.M." I want to know what you are doing, not planning to do.

If you tell me you are walking every day for thirty minutes or taking the stairs instead of the elevator or have stopped eating French fries because you are serious about your health, then I'm on your side.

Show me what you are doing. Not talking about doing, not planning to do, not hoping to do, not thinking about doing, but actually doing.

Sorry, but you don't know enough yet.

I want to get this idea out of the way right now. You are probably thinking it anyway, so let's get it out in the open. Regardless of how much you study, how much you learn or how much you already know, you probably believe you still don't know enough to reach your goal. You are right. You don't know everything you need to know to reach your goal. However, you know enough to start working toward it. That's all you really have to know: just enough to start.

> "You don't have to be good to start,
> but you do have to start to be good."
> **Unknown**

Fake it 'til you make it.

Surprised I would make that statement? It sounds like I am telling you to be a fake even though I preach authenticity at every turn. I am not telling you to be a fake, I am telling you to act with confidence, even though it is unearned, unwarranted confidence. Act confidently until by doing it, you actually own the confidence.

You can work on your confidence in many ways that have little to do with your actual ability to accomplish the task.

Learn the lingo when you set out to do something. Knowing how to talk the talk is an important step toward learning how to walk the walk. Want to play tennis? You better start by learning tennis terms like *love, service line, no-man's-land, match point* and *groundstroke* so you won't appear the idiot when you go out to play. The very least you can do is learn the proper language. Not to know shows a lack of respect for the task at hand. Now, grab a football bat and let's go tee up an ace!

Dress like you know what you're doing. Just like in junior high school when you went to gym class: You have to suit up. You have to dress for the part you want. A cop wouldn't get the same respect if he weren't wearing the uniform. The uniform instills respect. A uniform represents a commitment to the task. I think that's why referees wear striped shirts. It's why the military wears ribbons and medals on their uniforms to show what they have accomplished. It's part of the image. You have to create the right image while on your way to mastering the task.

When I was first learning to play golf, I bought the right clothes so I wouldn't look like a goober when I went out to play. Did it help me play better? No, but at least I didn't look like an idiot in addition to playing like one.

Carry yourself like you know what you're doing. I remember the first time I ever went to New York City. A friend and I went there for a business meeting when I was in my early twenties. I was such a rube. I was a country boy from Oklahoma who had never been to the big city. I walked around with my head tilted up toward the sky, sounding like Gomer Pyle saying, "Golllllly! Look how tall those buildings are!" My buddy and I were walking down the street one evening when a New York City cop stopped us and asked us where we were from. When we told him we were from Oklahoma, he nodded knowingly and told us to catch a cab and go back to our hotel. When I asked him why, he told me because we were going to get hurt walking around that area at that time of evening. We were astounded. I said, "But look around, there are little old women walking around all alone. Why can't the two of us walk around?" The cop said that those little old women looked like they knew what they were doing. They looked like they belonged and no one would mess with them. We looked like we didn't belong and didn't know what we were doing and we were targets for all kinds of crime. We got a cab and went back to our hotel. I learned a valuable lesson. Look like you belong and like you know what you are doing even when you don't.

Have the right equipment. When you go to the bowling alley, they give you a pair of shoes to wear and a bowling ball to roll down the alley. Unless you are an avid bowler and bring your own stuff, of course. But even if you are an avid bowler, the first time you went bowling, they issued you the right equipment. You didn't know how to bowl, but if you had the equipment, you could at least fake it until you learned how. If you didn't have the right equipment, you would look like a complete idiot.

Why was getting the equipment important? Bowling requires the right shoes so you won't fall down on the slick wood floor and bust your butt. Plus it requires a ball to roll down the alley to knock down the pins. It's hard to roll a block of wood, or a crowbar or a log; that's why you get a ball. Besides, if they gave you a log, it would be called logging, and that's something totally different. However, they don't give you a bowl either, and it's still called bowling—figure that one out! But I digress. The point is, you get the right equipment. Same with golf. Same with any profession. Landscapers don't show up to mow a yard with a pair of scissors. A cop doesn't chase the bad guys without a gun—unless you are in England, where the cops (called bobbies) get a stick.

Life also requires that you have the right equipment. Look around your house and decide whether you have the right equipment for success. Do you have books on success? You have at least one; you are holding it right now. Do you have others? You want to be more financially intelligent. Do you read the money section of the newspaper? Do you watch any of the money shows? Decide what you want to do and what you want to be and get the right equipment to make it happen.

Find a successful person and emulate his actions. You still won't have conquered the task, but you will be following the example of someone who knows what he is doing.

My buddy Brad is a scratch golfer. He says that when he first started, he told a friend of his who was really good that he wanted to follow him around and study what he did. The friend agreed. Brad didn't even take clubs. He just watched how this guy did everything. He studied how to approach the ball in the tee box. How to line up the ball on the green. Which club to use and when to use it. Brad asked his friend why he made every move he made. Brad took notes. He then started playing according to those notes. After a lot of practice, he started playing well. How? He found a successful person to emulate, studied how it was done and took action on his education.

When you find a successful person to emulate, don't argue with her. Nothing is more irritating to someone who is successful than to have someone who is unsuccessful argue about what it takes to be successful. Show some respect. This person is willing to share her experience and expertise with you. Be grateful.

Does faking it work?

Just last night, I was watching an episode of one of my favorite television shows, *The Next Food Network Star.* Yeah, I like the Food Network. I would love to have a cooking show of my own. I am one helluva cook! The premise of the show is, a group of wannabe chefs are trying to impress a panel of cooking experts to prove they have the ability to host their own Food Network show. Obviously, they have to be able to cook, but they also have to have some personality, since it's television. They were doing a challenge where they had to "sell" certain technical tasks to the viewing audience. They were assigned various things like how to shuck an oyster, how to truss a chicken, how to peel a pineapple and other things. One guy was assigned the task of opening a coconut. He went on camera with a nail and a hammer and began to explain exactly how to do it. I was sold. In fact, I was so convinced by his demonstration that I just knew I could do it the next time I needed to. I didn't know until it came time for the experts to comment that he wasn't doing it correctly at all. However, they said he had such confidence in his approach and was able to "sell" it so well that he ended up winning that competition. He faked it. But he made it.

Faking it only works for a little while.

Sooner or later, however, you do have to actually make it. You are allowed to fake it only while you are obtaining the skills to do it. You have to be able to act like a successful person while you are on the way to becoming a success. You have to have the actions of a rich person while you are on your way to becoming rich. You have to fake being healthy while you are on your way to becoming healthy. As you do this, you will acquire the habits of a successful, wealthy, healthy person. Who has the habits of a successful person? A successful person. See how it works? Cool, huh? By faking it until you make it, you will have moved from pretending to authenticity.

THE EASIEST ACTION PLAN OF ALL

Do anything that's different from the way you have been doing it. Read that line again because it's that important. Do anything that's different from the way you have been doing it. I mean anything. If your life isn't going the way you want it to go, any change will be a positive change. Any change in your actions will make a change in your results.

Your results are the result of your actions. If you don't like your results, you have to change your actions. This simple little idea is the key to your new life. Change what you have been doing and you will change what you have been getting.

"What do I change?" Again, change anything. Maybe change everything. If my results sucked, I would switch sides of the bed I sleep on. Would that work? Beats me, but it couldn't hurt. It might make me uncomfortable enough that I would wake up earlier and get my day started a little earlier. That certainly couldn't hurt.

> *Any change in behavior*
> *will bring about a change in results.*

Any new action is the right action.

Don't get all caught up worrying about taking the right action. Even if you wind up taking the wrong action, you will find out quickly that it was the wrong action. Then you can make the correction and take the right action.

Action is like a ball rolling downhill. The momentum builds. As you get started, one action will lead to another, and that action will lead to another, and before you even realize it, you will have accomplished something significant.

"I'm afraid to get started."

Years ago, I read a great little book called *Feel the Fear and Do It Anyway* by Susan Jeffers. Read the book when you can, but just internalize the title for right now. You are going to be afraid. No way around it. I am afraid quite a bit of the time. Yep, even me. When I appeared on CNBC's *The Millionaire Inside* as one of the world's leading money mentors, along with David Bach, Jennifer Openshaw, Keith Ferrazzi and Robert Kiyosaki, I felt some fear. I am totally confident when I walk onstage to do my speaking no matter who the group is or how big the group is or what topic I am going to speak about. I never think twice about it. When I was shooting my show, *Big Spender*, I was always confident in what I was going to do and I never broke a sweat over the experience. However, this was different. I was in a foreign environment with renowned experts, and I was going to need to hold my own on the topic of money. My heart was beating a little hard. Despite the internal questions I had about my ability, I walked out on that stage with confidence, grabbed a stool and did quite well. In fact, looking back at it all, I was pretty amazing. I was scared, but I blew through the fear and conquered the situation. I felt the fear, but I did it anyway.

While I am often afraid of what I have to do, I am even more afraid of not doing it. Earlier I wrote about the ten ways people sabotage their lives, with one of those being not recognizing consequences. If there are no immediate external consequences for nonperformance, I create my own. No, I don't punish myself or ground myself for not doing something. I just create the consequence of disappointment. I am disappointed when I don't achieve what I set out to achieve. Not when I've done my best. I never beat myself up for doing my best. I am only disappointed in myself when I have done less than my best. However, I am most disappointed when I don't achieve something simply because I have been too afraid to even give it a shot.

> To begin a journey and not make it is forgivable.
> Not to begin the journey at all is unforgivable.

What is the worst that could happen?

This is the question I always ask myself when I am afraid to do something. If the worst that can happen is, "I'm going to die," then I don't do it. But that is rarely the answer to anything I am going to attempt. Usually the worst that can happen is that I won't do as well as I had hoped. Or I might embarrass myself.

Is that really so bad? Even if I do it and do it badly, it is better than if I had never attempted it. So I go for it. You aren't going to die from going after more success, happiness and prosperity either. Ask yourself, "What's the worst that could happen?" Then go for it. Besides, the worst thing that could happen rarely happens anyway.

Dara Torres, the swimmer, won three silver medals during the 2008 Olympics at the age of forty-one. I watched her in an interview with Matt Lauer where the topic was her age in comparison to other Olympic contenders. She said, "The water doesn't know what age you are, so just jump in and go for it." The same applies to you as well. Life doesn't know, or care, how old you are or what other excuse you are clinging to, so just jump in and go for it.

Don't worry that you don't know everything. Don't get caught up in what might happen or might not happen. Don't be paralyzed by fear. Don't concern yourself with what others think. In fact, don't overthink the decision at all. When an antelope hears a lion roar, he doesn't continue to graze and think about whether he should run or not. He runs. No thought is involved. He instinctually moves. Become like the antelope because the lion is roaring. Move. Make taking action instinctive.

> *"The way to do things is to begin."*
> Horace Greeley

When should I start?

A guy goes to his retirement party. His friends are talking to him about his plans for retirement. He says he wants to travel more with his wife, to play golf and to spend time with his grandchildren. They commend his plans.

They all get together about a year later and are talking

about how he is enjoying his retirement. He says that he and his wife have been traveling all over the country, plus they have been to Mexico and Canada and even have a big trip planned to Europe. He also says that he has been playing lots of golf and has shaved five strokes off his golf game. He tells them that there is really only one thing he set out to do as a part of his retirement that he hasn't been able to do, and that is to play with his grandchildren. When his friends ask why he hasn't been able to do that, he replies that he doesn't actually have any grandchildren. They ask him why not and he says that he doesn't really know why he doesn't have any grandchildren, because he has three adult children who are all happily married and perfectly healthy.

He then comes up with a plan to get some grandchildren. He calls his kids and their spouses over to his house on Thanksgiving Day. He has them all standing around the table when he says, "Before I say the blessing, I have one quick announcement: Today I opened up a one hundred thousand dollar trust fund in the name of my very first grandchild. Will you please bow your heads?" He said the blessing, and when he looked up, it was just him and his wife standing there.

The moral? If you are ever going to get started, you ought to get started right now.

SECTION TWO

THE IDIOT FIXES

CHAPTER FOUR

TAKE ACTION FOR SUCCESS

Action changes things. I have beaten that horse long enough, don't you think? Maybe not, because no matter how much I say it, there are people who are still going to believe they can talk their way to success or think their way to riches and happiness.

Maybe it is time that I stop talking about the need for action and instead actually give you some actionable steps you can take. In this section, I am going to show you several areas of life where most people have problems. Then I am going to give you a list with specific steps you can take to turn things around. Some of the steps are extremely simple. Some of them are more complex. Some will apply to you and your situation. Some won't. Take what you need and use it. Leave behind what you don't need until you do need it.

DON'T ATTEMPT TO DO TOO MUCH.

Perhaps the enormity of the situation you face seems overwhelming to you. Don't allow yourself to be overwhelmed; instead, just be whelmed. Pick a couple of areas to begin with and get started on those. How do you know where to start? It's easy. What is most important to you? Is it your finances? Is it your family? Is it your weight? Your health? Determine what is most important to you and go take action on the area where you need to start making changes today.

"But what if I do everything on the list and it doesn't work?"

I admit that this is not impossible, though I can't see how it would be very likely to happen. Each item on each list is a positive action step to take in your life. Do just one of the things on one of the lists, and life will be a little better for you. String them all together and you should see amazing results.

Approach my lists with skepticism if you must. That's not an unhealthy way to approach any area of self-improvement. But in your skepticism, I want you to be willing to give a few of the lists a shot. At least give a few items on the list a shot. Will you fail? Possibly. But it is better to fail while trying to improve your life than to guarantee your failure by not trying at all.

THE FIRST LIST THAT EVERY OTHER LIST BEGINS WITH

1. Decide to change.

When I was in the eighth grade, after being humiliated for having only one pair of blue jeans, I decided to become rich. That decision shaped the rest of the decisions I would go on to make in my life.

When I went bankrupt and lost my telecommunications company, I decided to become a professional speaker. That decision is the reason you are reading this book today.

When my wife and I had marital problems, we decided to stay together. It was tough and sometimes felt nearly impossible, but making that decision and not wavering from it made it end in a healthier marriage.

When I decided to write my first book and sell it to a publisher, I also made the decision that I would do everything within my power to make it a bestseller. That book hit number one on the *Wall Street Journal* bestseller list.

Every good thing that has happened in my life has been the result of my decision to make it happen. The same applies to you and your life. Your decisions will shape your future. As you go through the steps I outline to do more, be more and have more in your life, understand that the list alone won't change things. You must decide that you are willing to do whatever it takes to live the life you want and the life you deserve.

> *"Always bear in mind that your own resolution to succeed is more important than any other thing."*
> Abraham Lincoln

2. Know why it is important for you to change.

Explanations of how to do just about anything are easy to come by these days. Go to Google and type in "How do I [*fill in the blank*]" and you will have dozens of answers show up, telling you just how to do it. The "how to" behind doing things isn't much of a mystery any longer. But *how* to do something is not nearly as important as *why* it is you want to do something.

There are literally thousands of books that describe how you can get rich. I say it doesn't matter how you do it, but it does matter why you do it. If you decide to get rich because you think you deserve it, that is a strong why. If you are doing it for your family, because you believe your family deserves the best, then that is an even stronger why.

I worked with a woman on *Big Spender* who told me her sole reason for wanting to turn her life around, stop her excessive spending and begin saving was because she wanted to be an example for her eleven-year-old daughter. She wanted to be an example her daughter could be proud of. That was her why. That is what kept her motivated when it got tough. She just kept reminding herself of the importance of teaching her daughter good fiscal responsibility. That kept her on track.

I watched many people fail at turning their lives around financially while I was shooting that television show. The people who failed were the ones who didn't have a strong enough reason not to fail. Their why wasn't strong enough to keep them motivated.

When I ask you to take a minute and think about why you want to lose weight, do it. That is an easy one: You want to look better, you want to feel better and you want to live longer. Some of the others will require a bit more thought. You will be tempted to skip them. Please don't. You need to ask yourself why you want to have more fun or be a better employee, be happier or take responsibility. That one question, "Why?" will help you determine if you even want to begin the task. Knowing why is the incentive for beginning and for sticking with it when the going gets tough.

I am about to give you several lists on how to be more successful in a variety of areas. I can give you the *how*. You must supply the *why*. With each of the following lists, I am going to give you a few lines afterward where you can write why accomplishing this is important to you. Don't roll your eyes and say, "Oh, boy, more lists!" These lists are important because they will help you define why you want to do something. When you get bogged down in the process of becoming more, it's the why that will keep you motivated.

3. Be willing to do whatever it takes to change.

Many years ago, I read a great book by Mike Hernacki, called *The Ultimate Secret to Getting Absolutely Everything You Want*. The book is still around and you should read it. Let me give the condensed version in a few sentences. According to Mike, the ultimate secret is that you have to be willing to do whatever it takes to get everything you want. Profound? I believe it is.

He says something in the book that is even more profound. He says that life rarely actually asks you to do whatever it takes, but life always asks you to be *willing* to do whatever it takes.

When I was shooting the picture on the cover of this book, the photographer told me a story of how several years ago, her business went through a slow time. To make money she hired herself out to shoot pictures of dance classes. She was used to shooting famous people and she knew this was way beneath her skill level, but there were bills to pay. She told me what was interesting was that as soon as she started doing the dance class photos, the rest of her business picked right back up again.

She showed a willingness to do whatever it takes. Because of that, she again became open to receiving more of the lucrative business she had in the past.

I know it all sounds like some cosmic mumbo jumbo and you are probably saying, "Yeah, right." You should know by now that cosmic mumbo jumbo is not my style. While the idea may sound cosmic, the results are real-world. The willingness to do whatever it takes opens you up to receiving more.

There was a time in my career when I was known as a motivational speaker. I even looked like a motivational speaker. I wore suits and ties and wingtip shoes. I had a regular beard and there wasn't any jewelry except for a watch and wedding ring. I didn't even wear earrings. Can you say *boring*? I could trot all that happy feel-good stuff out on the stage and get a standing ovation with the best of them. I could blow smoke up your skirt and make you just love your little pitiful self to pieces. I did it for years, was really good at it and made a lot of money doing it. The problem was that it wasn't authentic for me to be that way. After a good old-fashioned midlife crisis, I stopped being motivational and became the real me: irritational. I had to be willing to walk away from a very lucrative career and something I was known for, good at and respected for to switch horses in the middle of the stream and become a totally new and different product. I had no idea whether anyone would hire this new guy (the real Larry) or not. I didn't know what the outcome would be, but I knew I had to do it or go crazy. I was willing to lose it all to become authentic. However, I didn't lose it all. In fact, the willingness to become authentic made me more successful than ever. It made me more money. Most of all, it made me happy. I didn't have to do whatever it takes, but I did have to be willing to do whatever it takes.

Most people aren't willing to do what it takes. As John Wayne said in the movie *The Shootist*, "It isn't always being fast or even accurate that counts. It's being willing. . . . Most men, regardless of cause or need, aren't willing." John Wayne was talking about a gunfight. I have always loved this quote because I think it extends past gunfighting to every area of life. The most important part of the quote is the last sentence, which says, "regardless of cause or need."

I have worked with people who were in desperate need of money. I had a woman on my show, *Big Spender*, who refused to get a job because she had worked at jobs in the past and didn't find them fulfilling. She lived with her boyfriend, two kids and a dog in a two-bedroom apartment that belonged to her father, who was working three jobs to support all of them. Yet she wasn't willing to do whatever it took to provide for her own children. (I'm not even going to talk about the lazy boyfriend who considered his nine hours of work each week to be more than enough of a contribution.) I am rarely speechless, but when she told me this, all I could do was look at her and shake my head. I finally told her I couldn't begin to understand her position. If I didn't have a job, and my kids needed food or shelter, I would do whatever it took to provide. Hopefully, you would do the same thing. No job would be beneath me. The word *fulfilling* wouldn't even enter my mind.

While this might appear to be an extreme case to you, I can assure you it isn't. Every day, I see capable people who simply aren't willing to do what it takes to provide for themselves or their families. You see them, too. The street corners are full of people with signs saying they "will work for food," yet they aren't willing to get a job and work for the money it takes to buy food.

I have seen people puffing cigarettes through the tracheotomy holes in their necks because they weren't willing to quit smoking.

I have seen people after bypass surgery bellying up to the buffet to pack their arteries one more time because they simply weren't willing to give up the kind of food they like in favor of the kind of food they need.

Do you think these people don't know they are being idiots? Of course they do. They know what to do to change but aren't willing to do it. It is the willingness to do what you have to do that will carry you through to the next step.

> Life is not made up of the haves and the have-nots.
> Life is made up of the wills and the will-nots.

4. Do whatever it takes to change.

Being willing to do whatever it takes is a great step to take. Willingness alone still won't get you very far. You also have to *do* it. Yes, I know—I'm about to talk about taking action again.

"I'm not in the mood to get started today. I'll wait until it feels right before I start." We both know that is a total load of crap. You won't be any more in the mood to do it tomorrow or next week than you are right now.

Part of what I do for a living is write books. I promise you, there are many days when I am not inspired to sit down at my computer and type. I don't have it in me. I'm not in the mood. Sometimes, I just don't want to. I tell myself that I'll wait until I'm inspired and get it done then. Who am I kidding? I'm being lazy. Luckily, I know myself well enough to understand that, so

I just go ahead and plant myself and start typing. Funny that when I start typing, the inspiration seems to catch up with my fingers and it all works out.

> *"We should be taught not to wait for inspiration to start a thing. Action always generates inspiration. Inspiration seldom generates action."*
>
> Frank Tibolt, *A Touch of Greatness*

Good ideas don't get better with time. If you knew for sure that one of the ideas in this book could make you a million dollars, when would be a good time to start? How about next year? Does that sound like a good time to start making your million? I know you're broke right now, but why don't you wait a year until you are inspired and ready to get started. That makes sense, doesn't it? Sure it does!

5. When you fail, dust yourself off and start again.

Don't think your journey toward success in any area is going to be all smooth sailing. It won't be. I almost feel sorry for people who believe that once they get started, they will be fine and all will go well for them. These folks are naïve. You are going to make mistakes. You are going to slip up. You are going to fall off the wagon. You are going to experience setbacks and failures. Welcome to the world of growth. It happens. Instead of expecting it not to happen and being devastated when it does, be prepared.

Many people failed initially.

John Grisham, the famous novelist, had his first manuscript, *A Time to Kill*, turned down by twelve publishers and sixteen agents before it was finally picked up.

Michael Jordan, the greatest basketball player of all time, was cut from his high school varsity team.

Woody Allen, the Academy Award–winning producer-writer-director, was kicked out of film school for poor attendance and bad grades.

Elvis, the King of Rock and Roll, was fired after his first performance at the Grand Ole Opry and told that he wasn't going anywhere in music and should go back to driving a truck.

Babe Ruth, while once holding the record for home runs, also held the record for strikeouts.

Have you ever failed as a parent? Of course you have. I have plenty of times. Did you throw away your kids and give up? Stupid idea, huh? No, you just went back to parenting and tried to do better the next time.

When my son Patrick was learning to parallel park, he failed at doing it about a hundred times. He got so frustrated that he told me he just wouldn't drive anymore. Did he quit driving? No. He just kept at it until he got it right.

Failing at something means little in the big scheme of things. It certainly doesn't mean you are a failure; it only means you failed at this one attempt, this time. Keep going and you may make history.

Play through the pain.

Tiger Woods won the 108th U.S. Open golf tournament. In obvious pain from the knee surgery he had gone through just eight weeks before, Tiger sucked it up and reached down deep to pull out an amazing victory. Another professional golfer said perhaps Tiger wasn't hurt as bad as he was letting on. He implied that maybe Tiger was faking the pain some to garner sympathy and give himself an excuse in case he didn't win. It is so easy to criticize another guy when you weren't good enough to even be in the hunt. A few days after the tournament, it came out that Tiger had played with torn ligaments in his knee, and his leg was also fractured in two places. He would need to have more surgery and lay out the rest of the 2008 season. Doesn't seem like he was faking it much, does it? Tiger was in pain. Real pain. But winning mattered to him. He didn't offer himself or anyone else any excuses. He was pretty private about the whole thing. He gritted his teeth, winced in pain as he swung the club and won the tournament. I later read an interview with a friend of Tiger's who had accompanied him to his doctor prior to the tournament. The doctor told Tiger that he shouldn't play in the tournament because of his knee. The friend reported that Tiger's response was, "I'll play and I'll win." Tiger has since called that win the most significant win of his career. He could have skipped the tournament, and everyone would have understood. He could have quit in the middle and no one would have blamed him. Instead, he played through the pain to make history.

Setbacks will happen. Sometimes your journey will require you to play through the pain. The key is not to get stuck when it happens. Dust yourself off and start again. Regroup. Refocus. Don't whine. Think about what went wrong and why it went wrong. Don't spend a lot of time in analysis. Suck it up and go back to work. That's how you get there.

My philosophy on the process is this:

> *Expect the best.*
> *Be prepared for the worst.*
> *Celebrate it all!*

Which leads me to the next step:

6. When you get there, celebrate!

Have a little party for yourself. It doesn't need to be a party with other people and paper hats unless what you have accomplished is huge. Even then, I'd skip the paper hats. Just give yourself a little mental pat on the back, knowing you have accomplished something.

7. Move on.

When you mess up, it is important not to wallow in your misery for very long. Lick your wounds, but get over it all pretty quickly. You have to move on. This concept is equally important when it comes to your successes. Don't wallow in your successes either. Too many people experience a success and then sit back on their laurels (their butts) and celebrate their successes too much. The best time to get started on a new project is when you are high on the victory of your last project.

8. Become totally committed.

Why are you starting the task you have chosen? To finish it.
Will it be hard? Of course it will.
Will you want to quit? Oh, yeah.
Will you get there? If you want to badly enough.
How? Commitment.

When I become committed to do something, I do it. Period. There won't be an excuse good enough for me not to do it. It doesn't matter whether I have made that commitment to someone else or to myself. I said I would do it, so I will. It may not be convenient to do it, but I still do it. I may lose sleep to get it done, it may cost me money, it may be embarrassing and it may be the last thing in the world I want to do. However, I will do it because I said I would. That is the meaning of commitment.

That's how I achieve my goals regardless of what they might be. I become committed. I don't let anything stand in my way. The thing that stands in my way most of the time is little ol' me. Sometimes I have to kick myself out of the way and get it done in spite of myself. I have to examine the ten sabotaging behaviors to make sure I have conquered them so I can achieve my goal.

That's exactly what I want you to do, too. I want you to become committed to your task. So committed that no excuse will work. So committed that nothing will be insurmountable to you. You have given your word and you will keep it no matter what! When you have that kind of commitment, you will be able to do just about anything!

"Okay, Larry, I'll try!"

Not good enough. You aren't truly committed if you are only going to try. We both know that when you tell someone you are going to try, you are giving yourself an out for not doing it. When someone tells you they will try, do you really expect it to get done? No. You know they will give it a little effort—only enough effort to convince you they tried—but you don't really expect it to get done.

When you invite someone to a party and they tell you they will try to be there—do you expect them to show up? Exactly! Don't tell yourself you are going to try to reach your goals either.

> *A promise to try is a promise to fail.*

As you work through this section's lists on various topics, keep these eight steps in mind and use them with each endeavor.

As you begin each of the lists for success, remember that each starts with these steps:

1. *Decide to change.*

2. *Know why it is important for you to change.*

3. *Be willing to do whatever it takes to change.*

4. *Do whatever it takes to change.*

5. *When you fail, dust yourself off and start again.*

6. *When you get there, celebrate!*

7. *Move on.*

8. *Become totally committed.*

CHAPTER FIVE

ACTION LISTS FOR SUCCESS

SUCCESSFUL LIFE ACTION LISTS

To Take Responsibility

Taking responsibility is the most critical step toward success that you will ever make in anything you undertake, either personally or professionally. The ability to take responsibility for everything you are, everything you do and everything you have is the biggest challenge you will ever face in your life. However, it will do you no good to go any further with this book unless you first accomplish this major step.

How to Take Responsibility

1. Make a list of all the things that are keeping you from being successful in each area of your life. Make a list for why you are broke, a list for why you are fat, a list for why you are unhappy, for why your relationships suck and for every other area of life you want to improve. Go ahead and whine all you want. List every reason and excuse you can think of. Don't skip this step. Make the lists!

2. Go back to the lists and write your own name at the top of each list. You are the only reason your life is the way it is.

Nothing else on your lists matters. There are people who face much bigger challenges than you do, and they have still figured out ways to be successful. Throw your excuses out the window and leave your so-called reasons at the door. Instead, get to the root of all your problems: YOU! Besides, we are all dealing with the same lists. We all face similar challenges. Some people take the list and get rich. Most people take the list and stay broke. It's not the list's fault. It's your fault.

3. Go to the mirror, look yourself in the eye and have a little heart-to-heart talk with yourself. Say these words: "My thoughts, my words and my actions have created the life I am living. I take complete responsibility for everything going on in my life. I will stop blaming others. I will never again offer myself or anyone else any excuses. I am in charge of my life and my results from this moment on. I am taking control now!"

4. Repeat this little affirmation every day until it is ingrained in your psyche. Yes, daily. It works. Repetition of anything positive helps bring about the positive result you are looking for.

5. Remember this line: Affirmation without implementation is self-delusion. What does that mean? Saying the words alone isn't enough. The affirmation is a reminder that you are responsible. Now you must prove you are responsible by taking action to create the life you want instead of the life you have.

6. Live by this rule:

LARRY'S NUMBER ONE RULE FOR LIFE AND BUSINESS

Do what you said you would do,
when you said you would do it,
the way you said you would do it.

This simple statement is rooted in personal responsibility. Practice it, and everyone you deal with on every level will respect you. Every time you are tempted to slack off, do less or be less than you could, remember that you are a person of integrity who lives life by this simple creed.

WHY IT WILL BENEFIT ME TO TAKE MORE RESPONSIBILITY IN MY LIFE:

_____

_____

_____

_____

_____

_____

_____

_____

_____

_____

To Get More Done

1. Focus on accomplishment, not activity. Don't confuse being busy with being productive. Those two things have little to do with each other. It rarely matters what you are busy doing. It always matters what you get done.

2. Have a written plan of what must be done. Work from documentation, not from thought. Make your plan tangible by committing it to paper.

3. Refuse to become involved in anything that does not move you closer to the accomplishment of your goals. This one can be challenging, but stay tough. Just ask yourself this question: Does it move me closer to where I want to be or farther away from where I want to be? Answer yourself honestly and do only what moves you closer to your goal.

4. Become selective with your time. This means you have to get really good at saying no. When someone asks you to do something that doesn't fit your plan, say no. When someone wants you to spend your time doing something you don't want to do, say no. It's a simple process but sometimes hard to pull off.

5. Beware of meetings. Meetings are one of the biggest time killers in business today. Do all you can to avoid having them and attending them. Here are my rules for meetings:

   a. If the meeting doesn't have an agenda, don't have the meeting.

   b. Have your meetings standing up. They won't last as long.

   c. When you have accomplished the goal of the meeting, end it.

6. Complete one thing before beginning another. Don't have four or five open tasks. Get something done before moving on. Very few people can have a lot of irons in the fire. Multitasking rarely works.

7. Beware of the telephone. Don't let it interrupt what must be done. It's actually okay to let it ring and go to voice mail as long as you return your calls promptly. If you are on a phone call that is running long, the best way to get out of it is to say, "I know you are busy and I need to let you go." No one will admit they aren't busy. Say that and they will let you off the hook.

8. Beware of e-mails. Don't let e-mails on your computer or your BlackBerry rule your life. Few things must be dealt with immediately. Set aside specific times to read and answer e-mail.

9. Shut your door. Next time you stay at a hotel, take the Do Not Disturb sign and use it at your office. If your office is a cubicle without a door and doorknob, use a piece of tape to post the notice. The "open-door policy" that people love to brag about having is a stupid policy. People will wander by your open door and consider it an invitation to chat. They are much more hesitant to open a closed door.

10. Work when other people are not around: during lunch hours, before others come in and after they go home. People are a distraction—avoid them when you have something important to get done.

11. To get more done at home:

    a. Stand up. You get very little done when sitting on your butt. This is a simple suggestion and you are probably laughing at it right now, but you need to trust me on this one. Stand up and walk around your house. You will see a magazine that needs to be picked up or a pillow that needs to be straightened or a table that needs to be dusted or clothes that need to be washed or folded. You wouldn't see those things sitting on your butt in front of the television. Stand up and move around.

    b. Turn off the television. Just vow to go a few hours with it off. Calm down, it's only a few hours! It's hard to be distracted by a black screen. You might think you are going to go crazy, but I promise you won't. You might end up doing some work, or exercising, or having a conversation, or even—dare I suggest—reading a book.

12. Stay busy. I get more done by accident than most people do on purpose. How? I just stay busy.

> *Activity brings about more activity.*
> *Sitting on your ass just brings about*
> *more sitting on your ass.*

WHY IT IS IMPORTANT TO ME TO GET MORE DONE:

_____

_____

_____

_____

_____

_____

_____

_____

_____

To Set and Achieve Goals

1. Put your goals on paper. Fewer than 3 percent of people have written down their life goals. It is no wonder they don't end up where they want to be. It's like beginning a trip with no idea where you want to go and no map to get you there. You will only end up in a place you don't want to be.

2. Make your goals big and challenging. No one sits down and writes out a plan to have a mediocre life. A mediocre life is what happens when you don't have a plan. Goals should challenge you to be more, do more and have more. They should motivate you to greater things. Ask yourself what you would attempt if you knew you could not fail.

3. Have goals for every area of your life. Have goals that are physical, mental, spiritual, civic, family-oriented, career-oriented and financial. It will make you more balanced to be working on all areas of your life.

4. Be specific. Don't write that you want to have "more." Define "more." How much, exactly, is more? I have stood in front of groups and asked, "Which of you has a goal to have more money?" Of course, the hands would shoot up. I would then call one of the people who so excitedly said he wanted more money onstage and hand him a quarter. I would then ask the audience for a round of applause for this person who had just achieved his goal. They would just look at me, confused. I reminded them that his goal was to have more money and now he had more money. He had exactly twenty-five cents more than he had had just a few moments earlier. While that amount wasn't what he'd had in mind, he had still achieved his goal. Don't be guilty of setting goals that are not specific. I want to lose weight. Big deal. How much weight? I want more money. How much money? I want a bigger house in a better neighborhood. How much bigger exactly and in what neighborhood? Set goals in terms of minutes, hours, days, weeks, months, years, pounds, color, size, dollars, location and square feet.

5. Get personal. Make sure the goal is really *your* goal. You can't work with true commitment on a goal that isn't yours, even though it is a goal set by your boss, your spouse or your doctor. Your wife wants you to lose twenty pounds. Will you do it? No. You will lose the twenty pounds when you want to lose twenty pounds and not one day before. I have received countless letters from people wanting help for their son, daughter or other family member because they can see them headed down the wrong path and want to set them straight. I always respond by telling them that it's impossible to make someone change direction. You can't help someone change when they don't want to change or don't see the need to change. People change when they want to. They change when it's personal to them, not you. You are the same way. Your goals must be *your* goals.

TAKE A MOMENT RIGHT NOW AND WRITE DOWN SOME OF THE GOALS YOU HAVE FOR YOUR LIFE USING THE GUIDELINES I HAVE OUTLINED ABOVE:

_____
_____
_____
_____
_____
_____
_____
_____
_____
_____

6. Determine the information needed to achieve your goals. Do you need more education? Do you need to meet some new people? Do you need to free up some time? This step was covered earlier in the book. If you didn't do it, go back now and fill it in. But education differs from goal to goal, so be prepared to learn more in each area of your goals.

7. Determine what you can do to get started today. I didn't say to determine what you could do to get started. I added the word that kills most accomplishment; I added *today*. Always remind yourself of the acronym T-N-T, which stands for Today–Not–Tomorrow. Tattoo that line on your brain. Do not procrastinate; take action immediately.

> *It's better to look back at yesterday in admiration of what you accomplished, even if it's just a little bit, than to look at where you are today wishing you had done more.*

8. Don't think too much about how you are going to achieve your goal. Too much analysis leads to paralysis. Too much thought can create worry and foster fear and doubt. Don't overly concern yourself with how you are going to get it all done. Just get started and learn as you go. Action creates courage, and momentum keeps you going.

> *"Take time to deliberate, but when the time for action has arrived, stop thinking and go in."*
> Napoleon Bonaparte

9. Have a completion date in mind. When do you want to achieve your goal? Some goals don't have completion dates because they are ongoing lifetime goals. Things like being healthy or prosperous are not goals with an end but are a way of life. However, some goals do have time limits. "My goal is to pay off my credit card by June 1." "I will weigh ten pounds less sixty days from today." Those are the kinds of goals with specific time frames.

10. Focus on the accomplishment of your goal—not the activity. Accomplishment forces you to constantly ask yourself, "What am I getting done?" while activity asks, "What am I doing?" What you are doing is of little consequence unless it impacts what you are getting done. Think results!

11. Believe it can happen. You won't achieve your goals if you are constantly saying, "There is no way I am going to be able to do this!" You have to believe you can do it. Remember that what you get when you achieve your goals is not nearly as important as what you become by achieving your goals.

12. Have a celebration when you reach your goal. However, don't make your celebration conflict with your goal. For instance, don't celebrate your weight loss by eating a pie. That would once again make you an idiot. Celebrate weight loss with a new dress or pair of pants, something your fat butt would never have fit in before you lost the weight. Sometimes it is helpful to know what the celebration is going to be in advance of even beginning. A big payoff at the end can be a great motivator in achieving your goal.

WHY IT IS IMPORTANT FOR ME TO REACH MY GOALS:

A STORY OF AMAZING GOAL ACHIEVEMENT

The Cowboy Story

For several years I was employed at AT&T. When the company was going through deregulation in 1981, I opted to take an early retirement package and strike out on my own.

I left AT&T and started my own telecommunications company. I knew I was going to need salespeople to help me start and expand my business. I had a person in mind who was experienced in telecommunications, was familiar with the local market, was knowledgeable about telephone systems, had a professional demeanor and was a self-starter. I had very little time to train salespeople, so I needed people who could "hit the ground running."

During the tedious process of interviewing potential salespeople, into my office walked a cowboy. I knew he was a cowboy by the way he dressed. He had on corduroy pants and a corduroy jacket that didn't match the pants; a short-sleeve snap-button shirt; a tie that came about halfway down his chest with a knot bigger than my fist; cowboy boots; and a baseball cap. I thought to myself, "Not exactly what I have in mind for my new company."

He sat down in front of my desk and said, "Mister, I'd shore appreciate a chance to be a success in the telephone biness." And that's just how he said it: *biness*.

While I was trying to figure out a nice way to tell the cowboy that he wasn't what I had in mind, I asked him about his background. He said he had a degree in agriculture from Oklahoma State University and he had been a ranch hand for the past few summers. But that was all over now and he wanted a chance to be a success in "biness" and "would shore appreciate a chance."

As we continued to talk, it struck me that his entire focus was on his personal determination to become a success. To my surprise, I decided I would give this young cowboy a chance.

I told him I would spend two days with him and teach him everything I thought he needed to know to sell one type of small telephone system. At the end of those two days, he would be on his own.

He asked me how much money I thought he could make. I told him that looking like he did and knowing what he knew, the most he could make would be about $1,000 per month. It was a commission-only job and the average commission on the type of systems he would be selling was $250. If he saw 100 prospects per month, that would mean selling four of them a telephone system, netting him $1,000. He said that sounded good to him because the most he ever made was $400 per month as a ranch hand and he was ready to make some real money. For him, in the early eighties, $1,000 was real money.

The next morning, I sat him down to cram as much of the telephone "biness" as I could into a twenty-two-year-old cowboy with no business experience, no telephone experience and no sales experience. He looked like anything but a professional salesperson in the telecommunications business. He had none of the qualities I was looking for in an employee except one: He was focused on becoming a success.

At the end of two days of training, Cowboy (that's what I called him then, and still do) went to his cubicle, took out a sheet of paper and wrote down four things:

1. *I will be a success in business.*
2. *I will see 100 people per month.*
3. *I will sell four telephone systems per month.*
4. *I will make $1,000 per month.*

He tacked that sheet of paper on the cubicle wall in front of him and went to work.

At the end of the first month, he hadn't sold four telephone systems. Instead, at the end of his first ten days he had sold *seven* telephone systems. At the end of his first year, he hadn't earned

$12,000 in commissions as I told him he could expect to earn. Instead, he had earned more than $60,000 in commissions.

He was indeed amazing. One day he walked into my office with a contract and payment for a telephone system and I asked him how he had sold this one. He said, "I just told her, 'Ma'am, if it don't do nothing but ring and you answer it, it's a hell of a lot purdier than that one you got.' She bought it."

The woman had written him a check in full for the telephone system, but Cowboy wasn't sure I would take a check, so he drove her to the bank and had her get cash. He carried a stack of hundred-dollar bills into my office and asked, "Larry, did I do good?" I assured him he did good!

At the end of three years, he owned half of my company. At the end of another year, he owned three other companies. At the time we separated as business partners, he was driving a $60,000 black pickup truck, wearing $1,000 cowboy-cut suits, $1,500 cowboy boots, and a three-carat horseshoe-shaped diamond ring. Cowboy had indeed reached his goal and become a success in "biness."

What made Cowboy a success? Was it because he worked harder than other people? That helped. Was it because he was smarter than anyone else? I can assure you that wasn't the case. What was it? I believe it came down to these things:

1. **He focused on success.** He knew what he wanted and went after it.

2. **He took responsibility.** He took responsibility for where he was and then took the action needed to make it different.

3. **He had vision and goals.** He saw himself as a success. He had specific, written goals. He kept them in front of himself and went over them every day.

4. **He had perseverance.** He stayed with it even when things got tough. He never let a slammed door in the face slow him

down; he just kept knocking on doors until one of them stayed open.

Cowboy has made millions of dollars. He has also lost it all, only to get it all back again. He has been way up and way down. In his life, as well as in mine, again and again the principles of success have worked. Cowboy is proof that it's not environment or education or technical skills that make you a success. It's having goals and taking action to make your goals come true.

To Be Smarter

1. Read. Nothing is better than reading for improving your knowledge. Don't offer me any excuses about why you don't have the time—just do it.

The sad fact is, on the average, people spend twenty hours per week watching television and less than two hours per week reading. Fifty-eight percent of Americans won't read a nonfiction book after high school. Forty-two percent of university graduates never read another book at all after college. Only 20 percent will buy or read a book this year. Seventy percent have not been in a library or bookstore in the past five years. I guess these folks feel they have all of the information necessary to be successful, prosperous and healthy.

I worked with a business owner whose company was about to go under. I asked her what she did to prepare to go into business on her own. She said that she had passion for her product and that was all she needed. I said, "But what about education? What about being prepared? What about knowing what you are doing?" Nope, that wasn't important to her at all. She had passion! Yes, she did, but she was passionately incompetent. Now she was desperate and begging for my help. I gave her ten books to read that would help prepare her for running a business. I told her to read them and call me in a month to tell me what she had learned. I never heard from her again.

2. Get some books on the topic you want to know more about. Want to know about losing weight? Buy a book about exercise and eating right. Want to know how to get out of debt? Buy a book about that. (Start with my book *You're Broke Because You Want to Be: How to Stop Getting By and Start Getting Ahead.*) Whatever you want to be better at, someone has written a book that can help. Get a stack of books to read. If you still have a question about what to read, remember this: Find out what successful people read and read that. How will you know? Find a successful person and ask him what he is reading. Want to know what I'm reading? Go to my Web site and check out my blog. I am always doing a book review of the books that I'm reading. I even have a blog called "Five Books That Changed My Life."

3. Carve out some time each day for education. Don't say something stupid like "I don't have time to read." That's offensive to those of us who make the time to read. You have plenty of time to read. If it is important enough to you, then you will find the time to do it. That principle works across the board. Whatever is important to you, you will find the time to do. Begin with fifteen minutes. Everyone can find fifteen minutes a day to read. Start with fifteen minutes and build from there.

4. Use your travel time to listen to great books. Almost every great book today is available on audio either on CD or as an MP3 download. You can also *selectively* listen to the radio. Top 40 radio won't make you a better parent, spouse or businessperson. Howard Stern certainly won't. If you are going to listen to the radio, listen to a station where you are going to learn something. There is plenty of radio programming where you can hear interviews with great authors and other experts, such as NPR.

5. Watch good television. I love television. I try not to watch too many sitcoms and other mind drivel even though some are fun and I get a kick out of them like everyone else. But I love the History Channel, Food Network, A&E, Discovery Channel, TLC, National Geographic and some of the other great networks where you can actually learn something. Check out PBS, where you might even catch me talking about success on my special *Success Is Your Own Fault*.

My son Tyler, who is not much of a reader, has an education like few others because he "kills" time watching educational television. He can't tell you who is winning on *American Idol* or *Dancing with the Stars*, but he can tell you amazing things about life, health, food, history and nature, all from watching high-quality educational television. Television is not a substitute for books, but it's a nice addition.

6. Hang around smart people. Your income is likely to average that of your five closest friends. It's a fact. Think of your five closest friends and estimate what their incomes are. I'll bet yours is within 5 percent of theirs. Not happy with your income? Get richer friends. This principle applies to how smart you are as well. Smart people rarely hang around stupid people unless they are related to them. It also applies to how healthy you are and how happy you are. Fat people normally hang around other fat people. Happy people hang around other happy people—that is why they are happy. It's hard to be happy when you hang around whiney, sad, angry people! Get the picture? Are you hanging around the kind of people you want to be like? If not, dump them and get new people to hang around. By the way, if your friends start dumping you—it's probably because they read this section and don't want you as a friend any longer.

> *"Tell me thy company, and I will tell thee what thou art."*
> Miguel de Cervantes, *Don Quixote*

WHY I NEED TO LEARN MORE INFORMATION AND BE SMARTER:

_____
_____
_____
_____
_____
_____
_____
_____
_____
_____
_____
_____

> *"The man who doesn't read good books has no advantage over the man who can't read them."*
>
> Mark Twain

To Make Great Conversation

Ever been at a party and had no clue what to say to people? Have you ever left a party and said to yourself, "Those people must think I am as dumb as a stump!" I'm sure that just about everyone has found themselves in situations where they felt stupid because they didn't have anything to say to others. Here are some surefire ways to be more comfortable making conversation in any situation.

1. Read the headlines of that day's paper in the areas of news, sports, entertainment and money.

2. Find out what is on the bestseller list and read a review of the top three or four books. Even if you haven't read the books, you will appear smart because you know what they are and have read the reviews.

3. Read a few movie reviews. You can always say that you haven't seen the movie yet, but at least you will know what the others are saying.

4. Tune in to any of the news channels where you can get that day's news in just a few minutes.

5. Watch one of the entertainment news programs so you can catch up on the hot news in the entertainment industry. Even if there isn't anything you can use, you'll get a kick out of seeing what stupid thing some goofball celebrity has done.

6. Check the home page of your Internet carrier. They always have the top stories in several categories.

7. Just say, "What do *you* think?" about whatever is being discussed. People love to tell you what they think, and then you can just react to what they are saying.

8. "Read any good books lately?" "Seen any good movies?" "Did you see on the news that . . . ?" "I read in the paper that . . ." Ask lots of questions.

9. The weather, the food and the location of the party are always great things to talk about.

10. When you find yourself in real trouble, excuse yourself to go use the restroom.

WHY I NEED TO BE BETTER AT MAKING CONVERSATION, AND HOW THIS WOULD BENEFIT ME:

_____

_____

_____

_____

_____

_____

_____

_____

_____

_____

_____

To Manage Your Time Better

1. Use the trash can more often. Throw away more stuff. You are probably saving and filing way too many things. If it can be found anyplace else, you don't need it. Use a shredder; that makes throwing it away permanent.

2. Handle every piece of paper only once.

3. End every day by preparing a list of what must get done tomorrow.

4. Throw your To Do lists away. You have plenty to do without putting it on a list.

5. Get a To Get Done list. Concentrate on what you must get done instead of what you need to do. Focus on accomplishment instead of activity.

6. Have a clean desk and work on only one thing at a time.

7. Always keep a pen and paper handy. Don't trust your memory. Take good notes.

8. Get a junk drawer. If you have any question about whether something is going to be useful, put it in the drawer. About once a month, dump the drawer. If you can do without the stuff for a month, then it wasn't worthwhile to begin with and really was only junk.

9. Collect all of your junk mail for thirty days. At the end of thirty days, contact each company and ask that your name be removed from that company's mailing list.

10. Set aside a specific time for returning telephone calls and then really return your calls.

WHY I NEED TO BE ABLE TO MANAGE MY TIME BETTER:

_____

_____

_____

_____

_____

_____

_____

_____

_____

_____

_____

_____

To Solve Problems

1. Don't deny that the problem is a problem. Those people who say, "I don't have problems, I only have opportunities," are idiots. Some problems are not opportunities—they are problems. Recognize them as problems and deal with them appropriately. Denial is stupid and doesn't do anything but prolong the pain of the problem.

2. Understand that problems force you to grow, and anything that causes growth is a good thing. However, growth is painful. But not learning the lesson is more painful.

3. Look beyond the problem. This is a tough one, but try to see past the problem to what life will look like after you get through the problem. This can sometimes help you endure what you have to go through. The good news is that there is life beyond the problem—visualize it.

4. Break the problem down into small pieces and deal with the pieces. Problems seem overwhelming because they are sometimes too big to deal with on the whole. Break them down into smaller manageable pieces. For instance, if you are in debt, the overall amount may be overwhelming. But if you break it down into small pieces, you can attack it much more easily. Focus on that one credit card bill until it's gone, or on getting your mortgage current or on saving one hundred dollars. That way you are attacking the whole problem, but it doesn't seem so huge. Remember the old joke: "How do you eat an elephant? One bite at a time." That's the same way you should attack your problems.

5. Stop disasterizing the problem. Deal with every problem the way it really is, not the way you imagine it could get. The worst that could happen rarely happens. My little French bulldog, Butter, recently got very sick. We took her to the vet and he did a zillion tests and was stumped. He told us the only option was surgery to see what he could find. We went right past the surgery and created in our minds the worst thing that might happen. My wife and I disasterized the situation until we had her dead and gone. The surgery discovered that she had swallowed a small rubber toy that didn't show up on the scope or any X-ray. They removed it, and in three days she was her little obnoxious self again. If we had stayed in the moment and dealt only with the real problem, we would have suffered much less and saved a lot of unnecessary tears and agony. Yet I broke my own rule and created pain that I didn't need to go through. Deal with the problem as it really is.

6. Write the problem down. When you look at your problems in black and white, they rarely seem as bad. Like the previous step, this is a reminder to deal with the problem as it really is rather than how you imagine it to be.

7. Focus on the solution. It's not what the problem is that really matters; it is what you are going to do about it. So what *are* you going to do about it? That's where your energy should go.

8. Get help. Find someone who knows more than you do about solving the problem and ask for her help. Of course, this should come after you have tried to do all you can do on your own. If you come to me and ask for my help, the first thing I will do is ask what you have already tried. Any good resource would do the same thing.

WHY I NEED TO IMPROVE THE WAY I HANDLE PROBLEMS:

_____

_____

_____

_____

_____

_____

_____

_____

_____

_____

_____

_____

To Be a Better Communicator

1. Be a good listener. Being a great communicator is as much about listening as it is about talking. In fact, most people are much better at talking than they are at listening. Pay attention to what the other person is saying. Pretend it matters to you, even if at first it doesn't.

2. Establish and maintain eye contact. Nothing ticks me off more than someone who won't look me in the eye. Eye contact not only conveys interest, it establishes a trust factor.

3. Ask lots of questions. The best way to get information from another person is to ask questions. People will tell you just about anything if you will only ask.

4. Give good feedback. Nod your head and say things that let the other person know you are paying attention. This is especially important on the telephone when the other person can't see you and must rely on verbal feedback to know you are involved in the conversation.

5. Act like what the other person is saying is the most interesting thing you have ever heard. This one can be tough. I have felt my eyes glazing over from time to time when listening to some bozo telling me something I didn't give a crap about, but I hung in because it was the right thing to do. Plus, that person was probably paying me, so I felt obliged.

6. Don't interrupt. Let the other person make his or her point. Then comment. I know that can be a challenge. There are some people who couldn't make a point with their finger. If the person can't make his or her point and you are going crazy listening to the person try, then politely remove yourself from the conversation and find a better one.

7. Become comfortable with silence. Silence is not a bad thing during a conversation. Give people time to think and reflect. Trust me, they aren't used to thinking or reflecting, so when you experience it firsthand, enjoy the experience—you may be witnessing history.

8. If you don't have anything of relevance to say, then please be quiet. Don't prattle on with nothing to say just because you like to hear yourself talk. I know professional speakers who are like this. They are so in love with the sound of their own voices that the audience has quit listening long before they have finished talking.

**WHY BEING A BETTER COMMUNICATOR IS
IMPORTANT TO ME:**

_____

_____

_____

_____

_____

_____

_____

_____

_____

_____

HAPPIER LIFE ACTION LISTS

How to Be Happy and Enjoy Life

1. Lighten up! Don't get your panties in a wad.

2. Forget blame. You can fix the blame or you can fix the problem. Spend your time fixing the problem. I get caught up in this one myself. I like to point the finger of blame. I'm good at it. I know how to make a case to figure out whose fault it is better than just about anyone. After I've put energy into blaming someone, I feel a little better . . . temporarily, but I am still no closer to getting past the problem and on to the solution. I have found it is better to skip the blame and move to the solution.

3. Forget guilt. Guilt serves little purpose. You can't go back and change anything. If you have messed up, apologize and move on. Guilt alone won't make you feel any better. You will feel better only when you have made amends and moved on.

4. Forget luck. Some people count on being lucky in order to be happy or successful. I believe in luck. I believe that luck is where preparation meets opportunity. The lucky people are the ones who are prepared, recognize opportunities and take advantage of those opportunities. Instead of counting on being lucky, focus on being prepared.

5. Create your own set of circumstances. If you don't like the way things are going, change the direction things are going. You are in control. Refuse to accept your condition, and go to work to create a new condition.

6. Focus on what you need to do right now. Too much time is spent worrying about what happened in the past or fretting about what might happen in the future. The past is just that: passed. It has passed you by and is over, so move on. The future probably isn't going to be as bad as you imagine it to be. Focus on the present. It's all you've really got to work with.

7. Give up the constant need to be right. This one is a huge one for me. I like to be right. I don't think I'm alone in this; I think all of us enjoy being right. Pick your battles. Sometimes it isn't worth the fight. If fact, most of the time it isn't.

8. Scope up: Give up pettiness on all levels. Does it really matter if the toothpaste tube gets squeezed from the middle or the end? At a restaurant, who cares who had a dessert and who didn't—just split the check and move on. Don't be petty—it is so unattractive.

9. Be as healthy as you can possibly be. It's hard to be happy when you are sick. It is expensive to be sick. It is inconvenient to be sick. It's time-consuming to be sick. And as Tom Hopkins says, "To be rich and sick is stupid."

10. Compliment others. It takes only a moment to be nice to someone. "Good morning." "Nice dress." "Lookin' good today." "Good job." So easy to say. For you, it will be over in the time it took to say it, but for the person receiving the compliment, it can last for weeks.

11. Continue to learn. A mind that is challenged and involved is happier than a bored one. Read. Go to seminars and lectures. Watch educational television. Go to museums. Join a book club.

12. Rise above the approval of others. Develop the attitude "What you think of me is none of my business." I know this one from experience and can promise that you will be much happier.

13. Fill your life with activities you enjoy. I know that's hard to do when you feel like all you do is work, work, work. If you can figure out how to do just one thing every day that you really like doing, and then expand that time as you can, you will be much happier.

14. Learn how to relax. It doesn't take long. You don't need a whole vacation to relax. You need to find a moment every day when you can relax both your mind and your body.

15. Master the ability to forgive. You can't be happy when you harbor ill will or hard feelings in your heart. You can't be angry with someone and be happy. Get over it. I am going to give you specific ways to learn to forgive people later in the book, but in the meantime, know that you can't be happy until you forgive people.

16. Be generous. With your money but also with your time. Give to people who need what you have more than you do. And never think you have too little to give some of what you have to others. You always have enough to share.

17. Enjoy your money. I wrote a whole book dedicated to how to earn more, save more and invest more. However, it is just as important to know how to enjoy your money. This does not mean spending more than you can afford. I am not in favor of living beyond your means. I am, however, in favor of living within your means and learning to have some fun with what you have. To become rich and live like a pauper is stupid.

18. Don't look for things outside yourself to make you happy. Happiness comes from within.

I have a good friend who desperately wanted to buy a motor home. He was obsessed with it. His cell phone was full of pictures of the one he had picked out. He carried around the brochure for it. He constantly talked about how he could just hop in it and go where he wanted to go, when he wanted to go. He had the money and he had the desire, he just didn't have any support. His wife wasn't wild about the idea, and I couldn't muster much support either, as I can't imagine anything more painful than driving someplace only to end up sleeping in a traveling hotel room that I have to clean up. It would be way too much like "sleeping in a van down by the river" for me.

At the time, my friend was in a work environment that was driving him crazy. He hated to go to work. He hated the meetings he had to attend. He couldn't stand a good number of the people he worked with. He hated getting up most mornings, knowing what was ahead of him. Finally things came to a head and he decided it was time to leave. He was fortunate that he had lots of other opportunities so he wasn't going to starve or not have the money to pay his bills. I understand that not everyone is in his position and they can't just leave their jobs because they aren't happy. I am certainly not suggesting that you quit your job just because you aren't happy. Quit, but quit after you have something else lined up! However, my friend had the financial wherewithal to be able to leave.

I saw him just a week after he left his job. He was a new man. He sounded refreshed, relaxed and ready to conquer the world. His face was even more relaxed and less intense. I asked him about his motor home. He told me that he hadn't even thought about it recently. I pointed out that the motor home had been an escape for him from a job he hated. He had thought the motor home would make him happy. It wouldn't have. His job was making him miserable and the motor home would have been a temporary escape at best. Leaving his job made him happy, and he no longer needed to escape from anything, and that was why he hadn't thought of the motor home again.

We often look for things outside of ourselves to make us happy. Some people shop. Some people eat. Some people both eat and shop. They are fat—but they sure are dressed cute! Until you point out to them that the external things are still not bringing anything but a temporary escape, they will continue spending and shopping in their pursuit of happiness. When they realize that happiness comes from within, they will no longer have the need to look outside of themselves.

There are even couples who think that another baby will bring them closer together and restore their marriage. Babies are great additions to a family, but they do not bring couples closer together. They add stress, cost money some people don't have, take away time from doing things as a couple and more. Having another baby is not the solution. The baby is an external fix to an internal problem.

Don't look for external fixes to your problems. Your happiness is an inside job.

AREAS OF MY LIFE I WOULD LIKE TO BE HAPPIER:

OUTSIDE THINGS I AM RELYING ON
TO MAKE ME HAPPY:

WHY I WANT TO CHANGE:

_____
_____
_____
_____
_____
_____
_____
_____
_____
_____

> *"Folks are about as happy as they make up their minds to be."*
> Abraham Lincoln

To Be More Thankful

1. Make a Thankful For list. List things like your house, your car, your friends, your abilities, your stuff, your family and your job. Also list the things you wouldn't normally think of, like your health, what you know and what you are learning.

2. Know that regardless of what your situation is, you still have many things to be thankful for. Remember, it could always be worse!

3. Begin each day by running through a little mental "I am thankful" exercise. Just open your eyes and be thankful you lived through the night—many didn't. Be glad you have something to do and people to do it with. Wait, you don't have anything to do or people to do it with? Go find something to do and some people to do it with, and then be thankful you found them.

4. Remember that everything that happens to you causes you to grow in some way. Even the lousy stuff. In fact, especially the lousy stuff has a lesson in it. Be thankful for the lesson even when you find it hard to be thankful for the lousy stuff that caused it.

5. Remember the people who *really* have it bad. By comparison, you probably have it pretty good. (By the way, as long as you are thinking of those folks who really have it bad, why not think of some way to help them?)

WHY I NEED TO BE THANKFUL:

_____
_____
_____
_____
_____
_____
_____
_____
_____
_____
_____
_____
_____
_____
_____
_____
_____

> *"The more you are thankful for what you have, the more you will have to be thankful for."*
>
> Zig Ziglar

To Be a Better Person

1. Keep learning. If you aren't staying current, you are falling behind.

2. Be charitable.

3. Stay busy. Become known as a person who gets things done.

4. Live a life based in integrity. When you give your word, keep it. When you make a deal, do whatever it takes to make it happen. When you sign a contract, live up to it.

5. Be authentic. Don't try to be someone you aren't. You will hate yourself for it, and the effort to maintain the facade will exhaust you. Be real. Many won't like the real you, but that is better than having people adore the person who isn't you at all.

6. Don't complain and don't whine. No one wants to hear it anyway, and they have problems of their own they are dealing with. I wrote a whole book on this one: *Shut Up, Stop Whining & Get a Life: A Kick-Butt Approach to a Better Life.*

7. Be reliable, flexible, punctual, available and decisive.

8. Stand for something. Draw more lines in the sand. Be uncompromising in your expectations, your standards and your values.

WHY I FEEL IT IS IMPORTANT TO BE A BETTER PERSON:

_____

_____

_____

_____

_____

_____

_____

_____

_____

_____

_____

_____

_____

_____

To Have More Fun

1. Lighten up! You aren't getting out of this thing alive anyway.

2. Be willing to be the fool sometimes. The ability to make fun of yourself is critical to having fun. Take your job seriously, take your health seriously, take your finances and your family seriously, but don't take yourself too seriously.

3. Make a list of things you consider to be fun. I like to watch funny movies, read humorous books, play golf, go out for a beer with my boys, call a buddy of mine who can always make me laugh, paint a picture, wash my car and walk around the mall.

Those might not be fun things for you to do, but they are for me. I try to work a couple of those things into my schedule on a regular basis. Look at your list of fun things and figure out how to work them into your schedule regularly.

4. Set aside a portion of your income for having fun. However, only do this after you have given some, saved some, invested some and paid your obligations.

5. Buy yourself a toy. Not a big expensive toy but a toy like you had when you were a kid. Try a yo-yo, Slinky, or jacks. It's not how much money you spend, it's how much fun you can have. When my son Tyler was in Iraq, I sent a bunch of toys to him in Baghdad. I sent little soldiers that you throw up in the air and they parachute to the ground, and little balsa wood airplanes and yo-yos and Silly Putty, string that shoots out of a can and every goofy thing you can think of. My son told me that he and his army buddies got weeks of laughs out of those toys and that the toys made it fun to come back to the barracks at night after a long, trying, dangerous day.

6. Own a whoopee cushion and red socks. This works better for guys. We think farts are the funniest things on the planet. A crowded elevator and a whoopee cushion are a guaranteed recipe for laughter. Regarding the red socks: Buy a pair and wear them just one time and I promise you won't take yourself so seriously. For years I have said the epitaph on my tombstone was going to be: "He was a red-sock guy in a brown-sock world."

7. Ask little kids how to have fun . . . they know! In fact, if you do ask a little kid how to have fun, I bet they will say, "I don't know how, you just have fun!" Exactly. Little kids don't over-think things. Sometimes, you just have fun without overthinking it.

WHY I WANT TO HAVE MORE FUN:

_____
_____
_____
_____
_____
_____
_____
_____
_____
_____

"Sometimes a laugh is the only weapon we have."

Roger Rabbit

To Manage Stress

1. Stop trying to *manage* your stress. Why would you want to manage something that you don't want at all? Organizing it isn't going to help you deal with it or get rid of it.

2. Determine the cause of your stress. This is what I have learned about stress and what causes it:

*Stress comes from knowing what is right
and doing what is wrong.*

Do this quick exercise. Make a note of the single thing in your life that is causing you the most stress.

_____

_____

_____

Got it? (By the way, if you are planning to pass this book along to someone else later, you might want to be careful about what you write down here. You may have just written down your spouse's name, and handing him this book would cause some real stress!)

You know exactly what you should be doing about the thing you just wrote down. You just aren't doing it. Which means it isn't the thing that is causing the stress at all. Not doing what you know you should be doing about the thing is what is causing the stress.

3. Be willing to do what is right. Take a minute and jot down the right thing to do about the thing that is causing you the stress.

_____

_____

_____

4. Stop doing what's wrong. Take a moment to write down what you have been doing about the thing on your list.

_____

_____

_____

Doing the wrong thing is the cause of your stress. Stop doing that.

5. Get a pet. It has been scientifically proven that a pet can slow your heart rate and reduce anxiety. I can spend five minutes with my English bulldog, Ralphie, sitting on my lap, and life is much better. My anxiety runs off me like sweat on a hot day.

6. Learn how to meditate. You don't have to take a formal class on meditation or become a yogi master to meditate. Don't even concern yourself with the word *meditate*. If that word is just too woo-woo for you, then don't call it that. Just learn how to slow down for a few minutes and quiet your mind. I can do it by sitting on my patio with my dog. I can do it by walking around my yard looking at my cacti. I can also do it by walking down a crowded street in Manhattan. It is practicing the art of clearing your mind even for a few minutes to add perspective to your life or to a situation. It is becoming centered in the present and letting go of the past and the future for even just a few minutes.

7. Exercise. This is also scientifically proven to reduce anxiety. I'm not saying run off and join a gym, because chances are, you won't go and it will be a waste of money. I'm not saying drop everything and run to the mall and buy workout clothes and new shoes. I am saying you should do anything you can that makes your heart beat a little harder through physical exertion. Try this: Take a walk.

8. Stop worrying about what might happen. It rarely happens anyway, so why worry about it?

9. Give up having to have control over every detail of your life. There is an old saying, "God is in the details." Okay, then leave the details to God. Happiness is in rising above having to control every aspect of life.

10. Watch five minutes of any episode of *The Jerry Springer Show*. If you think your life sucks, look at these idiots! By comparison, you're probably doing pretty well.

HOW LESS STRESS WOULD CHANGE MY LIFE, AND WHY THAT IS IMPORTANT TO ME:

_____

_____

_____

_____

_____

_____

_____

_____

_____

_____

HEALTHIER LIFE ACTION LISTS

To Be Healthier

1. Read labels. Cut down on fat, salt, calories and products that contain words you can't pronounce.

2. Exercise regularly. I hit this a lot, but it can't be said enough. Do something every day that burns calories and raises your heart rate. Remember that you have to burn at least as many calories as you take in or you will end up a chunky monkey.

3. Take ten deep breaths at least three times a day. Oxygenate your system. There are lots of medical reasons that I'm not going to explain since I'm really not qualified. Just know that it is good for you.

4. Become HWP. Don't know what that is? Good. That means you aren't cruising the Internet dating sites or reading the personal ads in the local paper. (Okay, just because I know doesn't mean I am doing that either!) It means height–weight proportionate. Get that way.

5. Play more. Find something you enjoy and that you feel good doing, and then make the time to do it. You will live longer and be happier.

6. Don't smoke cigarettes. Nothing else needs to be said at this point.

7. Drink in moderation. A glass or two of wine has been proven to be beneficial for your health. For those of you who don't believe in drinking at all, rather than judge those of us who do, just keep it to yourself and choose not to drink. If you do drink, don't drink until you get drunk. You may think you are funny, but the rest of us just find you annoying. You are an idiot. And the older you get, the longer it takes to recuperate.

8. Practice prevention instead of searching for a cure. Spend your time and money staying healthy to keep from getting sick instead of the other way around. Most people spend all their money trying to get well after getting sick. That's backward and it's stupid!

9. Go only to a healthy, skinny doctor who doesn't smoke and who doesn't automatically prescribe a drug for everything that ails you.

WHY I CARE ABOUT BEING HEALTHIER:

_____

_____

_____

_____

_____

_____

_____

_____

_____

To Lose Weight

An expanded version of this list appeared in my book *Shut Up, Stop Whining, & Get a Life: A Kick-Butt Approach to a Better Life.*

If you are like most people, you have been trying to lose weight. I know you have because I have, too. You and I contribute to the $33 billion that is spent each year on weight-loss products. I'm tired of it all. Diets don't work. Pills don't work. These ideas work:

1. You are killing yourself by overeating. Get a grip on that simple fact and don't forget it. Suicide is looked down on in our society because a person kills himself instantly. However, no one thinks a thing about killing himself over the next thirty years one bite at a time. A friend and I were talking recently about the hypocrisy of a big fat television preacher who just keeps getting bigger and bigger. My friend said, "He's eating his eyes closed." Now, that's funny!

2. Stop putting so much food in your mouth. That's right—stop eating so much. While what you eat is important, how much you eat is just as important. Eat less. I don't care how healthy your diet is; if you eat too much of anything, you will still be overweight. Cut back on how much you eat. In other words: smaller portions.

Just this morning, I went to a restaurant for breakfast. I ordered a short stack (two pancakes). The short stack was indeed short, only about an inch high, but the pancakes were bigger than the ten-inch plate they were served on. They had enough butter on top to lather up a fat boy at the beach. Sadly, most people would ooh and aah and talk about what a great restaurant it was just because of that. In fact, it is lauded as one of San Diego's best places to eat breakfast. Yet I always wonder whether restaurants are being praised for the quality of their food or for the quantity. Seems like for a restaurant to be considered good in America, it has to serve ginormous portions—to hell with quality.

My wife and I ate at a popular Italian restaurant recently that everyone said was the best place ever! When they delivered our food, there must have been 10,000 calories in front of us. Seriously, there was enough food for six grown people. My piece of lasagna was at least eight by eight and four inches thick, enough to serve four people. It was disgusting. It tasted okay but, holy crap, no one person needs that much food! Yet if they brought only enough food to fill a person up or to be healthy, they would go out of business for being stingy and serving skimpy portions. Instead, they load you up with mediocrity and astound you with their huge portions. I have been lucky enough to travel all over the world—nowhere does this happen except in America. In Europe, the focus is on how good the food is, how tasty it is, not about how much of it you can stack on a plate. They don't concern themselves with calories . . . yet Europeans aren't fat like Americans. Why? Portion control. They simply don't put as much food in their bellies.

3. Fast food. What are they selling? It's not convenience and it's not price, because those places are seldom very fast and they certainly are not economical. I know you don't go to fast-food restaurants for their outstanding customer service. Those things are what they promise you, but it's not what they deliver. What you are paying for is grease. Why? Grease tastes good. Don't tell me about the salads and the low-cal menu. Most people don't eat from that side of the menu when they go to a fast-food restaurant. They eat from the high-fat, high-calories side. And cheap? Who is fooling who with this one? Don't be fooled by the 99-cent menu. That dollar will end up costing you way more in the long run when it comes time to lose the weight you gained by eating "cheap." We all eat fast food from time to time. I certainly do. The answer is, don't go as often and don't eat the bad stuff! And don't be an idiot; you know what the bad stuff is. Need a hint? If it's fried, it's bad for you!

4. French fries: tasty, delicious, scrumptious, tempting little fat sticks. French fries have no nutritional value. Give them up completely. Don't eat them. And please, don't buy them for your kids! What a horrible habit you are cultivating in your child. At home, if you like the taste of fries like I do, just slice a potato, place it on a cookie sheet with a little salt and pepper and put it under the broiler for a few minutes. No grease and it tastes just like a French fry.

5. Walk. It's free. You can do it alone. You can do it with others. It doesn't take a membership to do it. There is no special equipment involved. You can do it in any kind of weather. It isn't age-restrictive. It burns calories. You can take your kids and your dog. You can talk while you're doing it. It's good for you.

6. Don't get on the scales too often. Every couple of weeks is more than enough. If you weigh yourself every day, I promise you will get discouraged because weight doesn't come off every day. Furthermore, your weight can easily vary by a couple of pounds day to day just due to water weight. Give it some time. You didn't get fat overnight and you aren't going to get fit overnight either.

7. You are going to slip. Deal with it. In fact, embrace it. Yeah, that's not what most folks would tell you, but I'm not most folks. If you are dying for a slice of pizza—if it is a flavor you are truly craving—eat it. One slice, though. Enjoy it completely. You can't do it every single day, but you can indulge from time to time. Adjust tomorrow.

8. Willpower is overrated. It's very hard to deprive yourself of something when it is right there in front of you. If there are M&M's in my house, I will find them. I can *feel* their presence. I can smell them in the package, and if I am in the mood, I will tear the house apart to find them. The key to dealing with my M&M's obsession? I don't keep them in the house. Instead of relying on my willpower to avoid the temptation, I limit my access. Makes sense, doesn't it? Alcoholics shouldn't go to a bar because it's too tempting. Fatties shouldn't go to the ice-cream parlor. And M&M's can't be in my house.

9. Hang around people who eat right. I have already covered this one. If you hang around fat people, you will have a tendency to do what fat people do. What do fat people do? They eat too much and they eat the wrong things. Find some skinny, healthy friends who will encourage you to eat right.

10. Drink plenty of water. Gallons of it. It's good for you in so many ways—plus it fills you up while it flushes you out.

11. Remember there are no healthy, risk-free shortcuts to losing weight. There is no pill or surgery that is either healthy or risk-free.

QUESTION: Did you take a pill or have surgery to get fat?
ANSWER: No.
You got fat by eating too much of the wrong kind of food and

by not burning more calories than you were taking in. You will get fit by reversing that process. That's the only healthy, risk-free way to do it. Everything else comes at a price.

12. When you lose some weight, reward yourself with something new to wear in your new size. Take your old clothes to the tailor and have them taken in. If you can afford it, get rid of your "fat" clothes completely. Give them away to fat people who aren't willing to go through what you went through to lose weight. Don't think, "I'll keep my fat clothes just in case I gain the weight back." Remove this possibility from your life. You aren't going back to where you were, because you know better!

WHAT/WHO IS IMPORTANT TO ME IN MY LIFE THAT LOSING WEIGHT WOULD MAKE A DIFFERENCE TO:

RELATIONSHIPS AND FAMILY LISTS

To Have a Better Marriage

1. Make a list of everything you like about your spouse. Be very specific. This will remind you of the person you originally fell in love with.

2. Commit to telling your spouse one of the things on the list every day. This will have an amazing effect on your relationship. Here is the coolest part about doing this: When you remind your spouse of what you specifically like about them, you will see more of it show up. When I tell my wife that I love it when she gives me a kiss and hands me a cup of coffee in the morning, she does it more often. When she tells me how she loves it when I hear her car pull up in the garage and come out to help her carry things in the house, I listen much more closely to make sure I hear her car and I move a little quicker so I can help her. Reminding people what you like about them ensures a repeat of the behavior.

3. Make another list of everything you don't like about your spouse. Then throw it away. You can't do much about it anyway, so don't drive yourself crazy focusing on what you don't like.

4. Leave your spouse little notes saying how much you love him or her.

5. Laugh together often. My wife and I have always been able to laugh together. That has been one of the keys to our marriage. We aren't always happy with each other, and we may be in the middle of a big ugly disagreement, but we can still laugh together.

6. Go more than halfway. That old saying "I'll meet you halfway" may work when negotiating a deal, but it won't work in a marriage. You have to go way beyond halfway to keep a marriage working. You even have to go more than all the way. You have to go as far as it takes to get along, and then you have to go a little farther.

7. Become a better listener. Hey, guys, you suck at this. Women want to be listened to. Guys want to be listened to as well, but it just seems to be more important to women. Do it. Life will go much smoother if you will just listen.

8. Hug more. Gripe less. This is one of those short, simple lessons that has huge results. If it won't matter tomorrow, then let it go today. Hug it out!

9. Fight fair. Keep the fight/disagreement/argument about the issue and don't make it personal. Making it personal is not fair. Keep the fight about the subject at hand and don't dredge up things from the past that have nothing to do with the issue. That is not fair either. Fights happen in the best of marriages and are the basis of a healthy relationship. You need to be able to disagree openly about differing opinions. Anyone who says that they never fight with their spouse probably doesn't have much of a marriage.

10. Have lots of sex. When sex stops, the intimacy usually stops and the relationship will deteriorate. (A note to women: Men are pigs. Have sex with us and we will do whatever you want. We will talk—we will listen—we will carry out the trash. Don't have sex with us and we will still figure out a way to have it—it just won't be with you. That's the law of the jungle. Men want sex and a sandwich and a little sleep. We are uncomplicated that way. Most of the time, we can skip the sleep and we don't care that much about the sandwich either. Use that information to your advantage.)

11. Look good and smell good for your spouse. Take a shower before you go to bed. No one wants to snuggle up to a goat.

12. Don't put the kids in front of your marriage. Don't put so much effort into raising your kids that you neglect your spouse. Raising kids is the most important thing you will ever do in your life. You owe them your best. But there will come a time when the kids will be grown and will go away and you will be left looking at that person you are married to. Make sure that person isn't a stranger.

13. For the men: Put the seat down.

WHY I WANT TO BECOME A BETTER SPOUSE, AND WHAT I NEED TO DO TO MAKE THAT HAPPEN:

_____
_____
_____
_____
_____
_____
_____
_____
_____
_____
_____
_____
_____
_____
_____
_____
_____
_____
_____
_____
_____
_____
_____

To Find a Significant Other

1. Know what you are looking for in a significant other. Make a list of the attributes you would like your significant other to possess. Design the perfect partner for you on paper.

2. Become the kind of person that the person on your list would be attracted to. Ever heard the line "Opposites attract"? Sure you have. It's a lie. Guys, if you are a fat, broke-ass ignorant slob, then don't expect to have supermodels beating down your door to be with you.

3. Think about the kind of places a person you want to attract might hang out, and then go to those places. Is your dreamboat a religious person? Then the bar is probably not the best place to look: Try a church. Looking for a fashionista? You probably won't find him at Wal-Mart. Is your ideal sweetie fit and trim? Try the gym or a sporting event.

4. Be confident. There is no one who is not attracted to confidence. Women dig it. Men love it. Confidence adds hair, drops ten pounds and takes off ten years.

5. Don't give up too much too quick. Whether it be information or the goodies, hold something back. People want most what they can't have. Plus, it will keep you more interesting.

6. Be able to communicate. The basic ability to have a conversation is very important in attracting another human being into your life. Know how to listen and how to talk. Have something to talk about. See "To Make Great Conversation" on page 137.

7. Don't be afraid to go after what you want. If you meet a great guy and know you would like to see him again but he isn't picking up on the signals, communicate your interest and initiate the next meeting.

8. Don't think you can make someone into the person you want them to be. People change—but not often. It is damn near impossible to change someone. And the challenge is rarely worth the effort. Save time: Find the right person from the get-go.

9. Sometimes you have to compromise. Don't compromise on the big stuff, but the little stuff isn't that big a deal. So you like tall blondes and she is a short brunette. Big deal. Is everything else good? Do you share the same values? Same goals? Same interests? Then get over it. No one is perfect. You aren't perfect in her eyes either.

10. Have some good disqualifying questions. A disqualifying question for me would be, "What is your favorite kind of shoe?" If she says "Birkenstocks," there would be no reason to continue the conversation or pursue the relationship. Similar answers would be "athletic shoes, flip-flops, flats or something comfortable." If she says "stiletto, high heels" or better and answers with a designer's name, like Manolo Blahnik, then we could be a match. Otherwise, I'm not athletic, nor do I go many places or want to go many places where flip-flops are the perfect footwear, and Birkenstocks are for earthy types and that isn't my type. I like to go where you have to dress up and look "deadly." Heels are what I like, so for me, that would be the right answer. I'm shallow that way.

11. Know your deal breakers. We all have deal breakers. Stupid is a deal breaker for me. Bad table manners are also a deal breaker. An obnoxious laugh is another. I told some buddies of mine this and they said, "Are you telling me, if you found your soul mate who was drop-dead gorgeous, but she had an obnoxious laugh, couldn't spell and smacked her lips while she ate that you wouldn't hook up with her?" Absolutely, because she wouldn't be *my* soul mate.

CHANGES I NEED TO MAKE IN MY LIFE TO FIND A SIGNIFICANT OTHER, AND WHY THAT IS IMPORTANT TO ME:

_____

_____

_____

_____

_____

_____

_____

_____

_____

_____

To Forgive Others

1. Make a list of everyone you feel has wronged you. Write down every name that comes to mind, regardless of how insignificant it may seem.

2. Be sure to include your own name. You will forgive others to the same extent that you forgive yourself.

3. Go down the list and work through the pain of each wrong. Don't relive the wrong itself. Move through it as best you can. Answer this as you do the exercise: Does it really matter all that much at this point? Chances are it doesn't. Be done with it and move beyond it as soon as you can.

4. Release the power that these people and situations have over you. Take all the time you need. As you are able to forgive, mark the name off the list and move on to the next name.

5. If you feel you must contact the person involved, think long and hard about it. It may not be in everyone's best interest to open up old wounds. Forgiving is a personal process that is more about you than it is about anyone else. If you absolutely feel that you must contact the person, be cautious. He or she may not remember the thing at all, or may have moved past it long ago. Reopening old wounds is rarely a good idea.

IT'S IMPORTANT FOR ME TO FORGIVE THESE PEOPLE BECAUSE:

_____
_____
_____
_____
_____
_____
_____
_____
_____
_____

To Be a Better Parent

1. Be consistent. If you tell your kids that something is wrong today, it should be wrong tomorrow and it should have been wrong yesterday. The rules don't change based on your mood, where you are or what you have time for. Rules don't have exceptions. If there is an exception to the rule, it was never a rule to begin with.

2. Make the punishment fit the crime. The punishment for running into the street should be different from the punishment for not picking up the toys.

3. When your teenager's room is a mess, shut the door. Save both of you the frustration of telling her one more time to clean up her room. When it is important enough for her to do it, she will—in the meantime, shut the door.

4. Don't cut your kids too much slack. You do your children a great disservice by being too lenient.

5. Don't be overprotective. Let your kids learn their own lessons by experiencing the pain of their mistakes. We all learn by experiencing the pain of consequences.

6. If you have little bitty kids, sit on the floor a lot. Physically communicate at their level. They will enjoy it, and it will do you good, too.

7. Don't expect perfection—especially when it comes to grades. Ask your kids to do their best, regardless of what that might be, and then be satisfied with it. Teach your kids to be satisfied with their best as well. Being the best isn't important, but doing your best is.

8. Teach them the really important things: kindness, charity, love, forgiveness, compassion, respect, honesty, how to take responsibility and how to have fun.

9. Teach your kids about money. How to earn it, save it, invest it and spend it. Remember, they learn by example, so be a good teacher by setting a good example.

10. Play with your kids at every opportunity. When they are grown, it is the playtime they will remember most.

11. Listen to them. Kids quit talking to their parents because their parents quit listening.

12. Ask more, lecture less. Ask your kids what they are doing, where they are going and who they are going with. Stay involved in their lives by asking lots of questions. Your kids won't always volunteer the information you want or need. You have to ask to get it.

13. Hug more. Hug your kids even when they think they are too big for it.

14. Respect your children's privacy. Yes, you have the right as their parent to know everything that is going on in their lives. If they have done something that warrants inspection, then inspect. But give your kids some private time as well. Everyone needs privacy.

15. Encourage your children to develop their uniqueness. Don't try to mold their personalities. Let them be who they are and not who you want them to be.

16. Don't make a jackass of yourself at their sporting events. Being too much of a fan is embarrassing to them, to yourself and to all of those watching you. Which means don't be obnoxious to the other team, or to the coaches, or to other parents or officials.

17. Your kids are going to want to dress weird. They are going to have strange hair. They are just trying to discover themselves and be unique. Don't worry about it too much. Green hair grows out. They will abandon their weirdness as they grow out of it. And remember, they will grow out of it.

18. Know your kids' friends and have them over to your house. Better to have a house full of rowdy kids than to wonder where your children are.

WAYS MY FAMILY AND I WOULD BENEFIT FROM MY BEING A BETTER PARENT, AND WHY THAT IS IMPORTANT TO ME:

_____

_____

_____

_____

_____

_____

_____

_____

_____

_____

To Deal with Jerks

1. Keep things in perspective. Remember that sometimes you are a jerk, too.

2. You can't change the way other people are; you can only change the way you respond to them. Why drive yourself crazy? Lighten up.

3. Know that it's rarely personal. Most of the time, you will have done nothing to incite a jerk's behavior.

4. Forgive them; they can't help it. Most jerks have received years of training to get good at it.

5. Be more understanding, because maybe they are just having a bad day. Determine whether it's a bad day or consistently inappropriate behavior.

6. Don't give them the power to ruin your day. They're jerks, remember? Don't reduce yourself to their level.

7. Be nice. Jerks hate that and will sometimes stop being jerks just to spite you.

8. Know that most people aren't really jerks; they just act in jerky ways. Deep down, I think, most people are good folks but work hard to cover it up. Their actions might make you think they are jerks but they really aren't. Attack their jerky actions but give the person a chance.

THE BENEFITS OF LEARNING TO DEAL EFFECTIVELY WITH JERKS, AND WHY I EVEN CARE:

_____

_____

_____

_____

_____

_____

_____

_____

_____

To Be a Better Friend and to Have Better Friends

1. Don't worry about how many friends you have. It is better to have a few really good friends you can count on than a bunch of fair-weather friends who won't be there when you need them. Go for quality versus quantity.

2. Make a list of friends called your Mexican Jail Friends. These are the people who would come to your rescue if you were ever stuck in a Mexican jail. And don't say, "That would never happen to me." Nay, nay, Eager Bunny, it might! I know exactly who I would call. My son Tyler, a cop, would be first. He would be there with a couple of his cop buddies with guns blazing! My friend and manager, Vic, would organize the whole event, rounding up the resources and coordinating the efforts to assure that the jailbreak would come off as planned. My speaker buddies would show up, get the jailers drunk, tell them jokes and baffle them with BS, while someone else actually did the work. My buddy Brad, aka The Damn Canadian, would probably be in jail with me, so he would be of no use except to keep me company. Who would get you out? These are your real friends. My advice is to be prepared.

3. You shouldn't have to work on your friendships. Friendships should be easy. If you have to work hard to maintain the friendship, then it isn't really much of a friendship. Friends accept you and let you be the way you are. They allow you to have your good days and your bad days. They let you be an idiot and make an ass of yourself. They will even let you whine. But they won't do any of this for long.

4. Be a good listener. The best friend you will ever have is one who will just listen. By the way, emphasis on the word *just*. This is why my bulldog Ralph is my best friend. No judgment, only a calm acceptance of what I am saying. He doesn't understand a word, but he loves me enough to just listen. Be like Ralph.

5. Friends should be tough on you. Let them be. Many people think that friends will put an arm around you and tell you how unfair the world is. Wrong. True friends will put an arm around you and tell you that you are an idiot. They will tell you that you can do better. They will tell you to stop being stupid and to do the right thing. They won't be soft on you, because they know you are better than the behavior you have been exhibiting. When they do this, love them for it.

6. When you mess up (and you will), be quick to apologize. Friends are hard to come by, so do everything you can to hold on to one.

7. Be quick to forgive. Your friends will mess up with you, too, so forgive them and move on.

8. Only have friends who encourage you to be more, do more and have more.

WHY HAVING STRONG FRIENDSHIPS IS IMPORTANT TO ME:

_____

_____

_____

_____

_____

_____

_____

_____

To Rid Yourself of Stupid People

You are a reflection of the people you associate with. If you aren't doing as well as you would like to be doing, you need to take a close look at your associates.

> *"He that walketh with wise men shall be wise."*
> Proverbs 13:20

> *"He that walketh with a dumb ass shall also be known as a dumb ass."*
> Larry's Proverbs 1:08

1. Ask yourself this question: Do these people move me closer to my goals? Don't lie to yourself on this one. This is a black-or-white area. People are either moving you closer to your goals or they are moving you farther away from your goals. Which direction do these people have you moving?

2. Ask yourself these questions: What do these people have me doing? Where do they have me going? What do they have me believing about the world? What do they have me believing about myself? What do they have me talking about? What do they have me reading? Are they satisfied with their lot in life?

3. Do the answers to these questions make you feel good about these people, or do they bring into question the quality of the relationships?

4. If you make a decision that these are not the right people to have in your life, then my first suggestion would be to buy them a copy of this book and earmark this section.

5. Be honest. Tell them that you are ready to step up to a new level of success and that they can either join you or you are going to leave them behind. This will be a tough conversation. If you simply can't have it, then try this next point:

6. Stop saying yes to being with them. After a while, they will get the hint.

> *"A man is known by the company he avoids."*
> Unknown

7. Become more than you are. When you do this, your old friends won't know how to react to the new you. They won't be comfortable with the fact that you are now expecting more from yourself, earning more, working harder and getting smarter. They will say that you are getting too good for them. They will be correct.

8. Don't spend much time looking back. Heartless approach? Not at all. You have to be true to your own dreams and goals and do the best thing for yourself and your family. Some friends are like belts: Eventually you outgrow them.

9. Enjoy the new friends you will make when you become more than you are right now. You will attract new friends. Don't worry about this one.

10. Know this is an ongoing process that happens throughout your life. You will always be saying good-bye to the old and hello to the new. It is part of the process of life. It proves you are growing.

Okay, get honest and write down their names and the reasons you need to get away from these people. A word of warning: If there is a chance a person whose name you write down might pick up this book and see his name, write down a code name. Use Heathcliff. That way, when people see it, they will wonder how you even know someone named Heathcliff. Unless, of course, that is the method you choose to get rid of this person. If that is the case, use his real name and leave the book out in plain sight and open to this page.

THE STUPID PEOPLE I NEED TO RID MYSELF OF, AND WHY I NEED TO DO IT:

_____

_____

_____

_____

_____

_____

_____

_____

MONEY ACTION LISTS

To Stop Being Broke

This is a much-abbreviated version of the money lessons I give in *You're Broke Because You Want to Be: How to Stop Getting By and Start Getting Ahead*. For a complete and comprehensive approach to a more secure financial future, read that book.

1. Figure out where you are financially. This means that you have to know exactly how much money you have on hand and how much money you earn after taxes.

2. Know exactly who you owe, how much you owe and when it is due.

3. Know what got you into the mess you are in. This means that you have to figure out how you have been spending your money. Make a list of your expenditures by going through your checkbook and your credit card statements and bank statements.

4. Know what you are willing to give up to get what you want. You have to be willing to sacrifice your lifestyle in order to make a change in your spending habits.

5. Keep track of every penny you spend. Get a notebook and write down where your money goes on a daily basis.

6. Sell all of the useless stuff you don't need. Garage sales, eBay, Craigslist, yard sales and consignment shops need to become a way of life for you until all unnecessary items are purged and you have raised some cash to apply to your debts.

7. Dump the gym membership you aren't using anyway. Give up the premium cable channels. Change your cell phone plan. Call your insurance agent and get a cheaper rate.

8. Stay away from temptation. Don't go to the mall. Don't go out to eat. Don't go anyplace that will tempt you to spend money.

9. Cut up your credit cards. Keep only one for an emergency. An emergency involves blood or broken bones. A sale at the mall is not an emergency.

10. Open up the lines of communication with your creditors. Don't hide from them and dodge their telephone calls. Talk to them. They want their money—you want to help them get their money. Work together to make it happen.

WHY IT IS IMPORTANT TO ME TO STOP BEING BROKE:

_____

_____

_____

_____

_____

_____

_____

_____

_____

_____

_____

To Save Money

Again, this is a much-abbreviated version of the things you can do to save money from my book *You're Broke Because You Want to Be: How to Stop Getting By and Start Getting Ahead*. For more information, read that book.

1. Don't offer yourself any excuses. Just decide to save some money and do it. Pick an amount that equals about 10 percent of your net income and start socking it away for a rainy day. By the way, a rainy day will happen, so it's good to be prepared. Cash on hand is always a good thing. In fact, I can't think of a time that a big wad of cash could ever be a bad thing.

2. Get a big jar and empty out all the change from your pockets or purse every night into your jar. A one-gallon jar holds about three hundred bucks' worth of change. You can easily fill one up each year by dumping your change.

3. Get a checking account that rounds up your expenditures and puts the amount in savings. You will be amazed how quickly you will save.

4. Enroll in all company-offered savings plans. Especially any that offer matching funds.

WAYS I COULD SAVE MONEY RATHER THAN JUST SPEND IT, AND WHY I NEED TO DO IT:

_____

_____

_____

_____

_____

_____

_____

_____

_____

_____

_____

_____

To Find a Financial Advisor/Investment Counselor

Never let an amateur handle your hard-earned money. I don't trust my money to amateurs and neither should you. This means you shouldn't be investing your own money. Unless you are an investment professional by trade, you are an amateur. Don't think you are smart enough to do a good job just because you read the money section of the newspaper or because you watch guys on television talk about where to put your money. Find a true professional to handle your money. Even then it's a gamble, but at least you will be gambling with a professional on your side.

1. Talk to friends about who they use. If your friends don't have a clue what you are talking about, then dump them and get richer friends.

2. Make sure your financial advisor has at least as much money as you have. How do you find that out? Ask. Make her prove it.

3. Before putting your money into any investment suggested by your financial advisor, make sure he has his own money in that investment, too. Make him prove it. If it is a good idea for your money, it should be good enough for his money as well.

4. Make sure the relationship feels good to you. If there is any question or distrust or something that you don't feel just right about, take your money elsewhere.

5. Investments are almost always long-term. A good financial advisor knows that. If anyone tells you he can help you get rich "quick and easy," he is a liar. I don't know one millionaire who ever did it quick and easy. It's always slow and hard to make millions of dollars.

BENEFITS A FINANCIAL ADVISOR WOULD BRING ME:

_____
_____
_____
_____
_____
_____
_____

BUSINESS ACTION LISTS

To Run a Better Business

For more about how to run a better business, be sure to check out my _New York Times_ bestselling business book _It's Called Work for a Reason! Your Success Is Your Own Damn Fault._

1. A deal is a deal. This is my number one rule for business. When you make a deal, you keep it, no matter what.

2. Do what you said you would do, when you said you would do it, the way you said you would do it.

3. Do the right thing every time. Not the cheap thing or the easy thing—the right thing.

4. Be the company your customers can count on to serve them well every time, without exception. Serve them with fair pricing, integrity, efficiency and excellence.

5. The customer is king. Treat your customers accordingly. Any company can survive without any of its employees. It cannot survive without its customers.

6. Never tolerate poor performance from anyone. Fix the employee's poor performance or set him free.

7. Don't worry about the competition. When you are excellent in every way, you won't have any. Just work faster, smarter and harder than anyone else is willing to work and you will own the market.

8. Run your business based on mutual respect among employees. It doesn't really matter whether you and your coworkers like each other or not, but it does matter whether you respect one another. Without mutual respect for one another's abilities and talents, you cannot work together effectively.

9. Every day, figure out ways to get more done with less. That means less of everything, including people. The companies that focus on doing more with less while still maintaining excellence will always survive.

10. Keep your workplace clean. Sounds like it shouldn't be that big a deal, but it is to your customer. Plus, a clean work environment is more efficient.

WHY I NEED TO LEARN TO RUN A BETTER BUSINESS:

To Be a Better Manager

This list appears in a much-expanded form in my book *It's Called Work for a Reason! Your Success Is Your Own Damn Fault.* If you want more information about any area of business, that book contains plenty!

1. Set clear expectations for every employee. Communicate these expectations to each employee. How can you measure an employee's performance when no bar has been set?

2. Be decisive. When it's time to make a decision, make one, then make that decision right. There is nothing that weakens a manager like the inability to make a decision. Just about any decision you make can be made to work out, so don't second-guess yourself and don't get stuck being indecisive.

3. It is not as important to be liked as it is to be respected. Being liked is just a bonus. Being respected is critical to your success.

4. Never mess with people's money. Pay employees well and pay them on time, as you agreed to.

5. Disrespect from an employee is grounds for immediate dismissal.

6. As the saying goes, if it ain't broke, don't fix it. But if it *is* broken, fix it fast. Problems grow and spread from neglect. When you recognize a problem, fix it immediately before it becomes a bigger problem.

7. A deal is a deal. Keep your word with your employees as well as with your customers. A verbal commitment should be considered the same as a contract.

8. When hiring, beware of articulate incompetents who talk a good game but can't deliver the goods. As soon as you realize you have been duped, dump them.

9. Fire people when they need to be fired. You aren't doing anyone a favor by keeping bad employees—not them, not you, not your customers or your company and certainly not your other employees.

10. Keep things simple. If things start to feel complicated, stop, evaluate and begin again.

**HOW IT WILL BENEFIT ME AND MY COMPANY
IF I BECOME A BETTER MANAGER, AND WHY
I WANT TO DO IT:**

\
\
\
\
\
\
\
\
\

To Be a Better Employee

This list also appears in expanded form in *It's Called Work for a Reason! Your Success Is Your Own Damn Fault.* The book contains many great ideas on how to get more from your job and how to be more successful in business, but here is a distillation of the essentials on being a better employee:

1. Focus on accomplishment, not activity. Be known as the person who gets things done, not the person who just looks busy.

2. It's hard to change your reputation, so develop one you're proud of.

3. Be trustworthy. Keep your mouth shut more often than open. Be a good confidant that others know they can trust.

4. Be punctual. Be there when you said you would be. No excuses.

5. Don't brag. Everyone hates a braggart. If your performance is recognized, be gracious in accepting the compliment.

6. Don't complain. No one wants to hear it, and they have their own problems to deal with, so keep your problems to yourself.

7. Friendship among coworkers is a bonus. It is not required, nor is it to be expected.

8. Ask your boss what the single most important thing is about your job, and then make sure it gets done. Every day you should focus on that one thing. Of course, that is not to say you shouldn't seek out other things to accomplish also, but make certain that one thing gets done.

9. Remember that you work for someone, and that person has the right to say what you do, when you do it and how you do it. You have the right to make suggestions, but your boss has the final say.

10. Do not tolerate abuse or disrespect from your employer. And do not stay at your job if your employer is dealing dishonestly or unethically in any way. There are other jobs.

WHY I WANT TO BECOME A BETTER EMPLOYEE:

_____

_____

_____

_____

_____

_____

_____

_____

_____

COMMONSENSE ACTION LISTS

To NOT Get Duped

1. When asked to give to a charity, find out what percentage of the money actually goes to the cause and not to the administration of the cause. If they don't know the answer to that question, walk away or hang up. If more goes to running the organization than goes to the cause itself, this is not a charity you want to be involved in.

2. If it sounds too good to be true, it is. Don't fall victim to things that sound too good. You have *not* been specially selected. A prince in Nigeria does *not* have $10 million being held in an account and just needs two grand from you to get it released and if you help him, he will share it with you. People actually fall for this stuff! Why? We like believing there is something other than work that is going to make us rich.

3. Ask hard questions. You work hard for your money; don't be afraid to ask a lot of questions before you share it with anyone.

4. Get it in writing. Never play "He said, she said." Your memory isn't good enough and neither is theirs. Go to the sheets of paper that everyone agreed to and signed and then live with what's on the paper.

5. Ask for references. Then call the references. Having references is one thing, but calling them is the key. It's amazing how many people never check references. A guy came to my door wanting to trim my trees. He said he had trimmed my neighbor's trees and the neighbor suggested he come talk with me about doing mine. I didn't buy it. Most of my own neighbors don't even know my name and would never sic someone on me: They think I bite! So I asked him to give me the neighbor's name and I would call to verify if what he was saying was true. The guy said he had it in his truck and would be right back. He then walked to his truck, got in and drove away. That's what I thought!

6. There are no real guarantees; you will still get duped. That's reality. You will be taken advantage of. You will spend money on things that don't work. You will be lied to. Companies won't perform as promised. You will get screwed. Just try not to let it happen very often.

WHY I NEED TO LEARN HOW TO NOT GET DUPED:

_____

_____

_____

_____

_____

_____

_____

To Dress Better

"How can a grown man who has two earrings, bracelets to his elbows, rings on every other finger, and wears blue jeans, cowboy shirts and boots have anything to teach anyone about fashion?"

That is a fair question. However, I don't always wear the shirts, jeans and boots. I also sometimes take it down a notch to just a few rings and even only one bracelet. The earrings stay, though. I am a student of fashion. Always have been. That's probably why one of my sons ended up a fashion designer. I like clothes. Plus, I pay attention. I know what works and doesn't work. So pay attention and heed some solid fashion advice. By the way, as always, my advice for both men and women is tough.

Fashion Tips for Everyone

1. Be careful what you wear in public. Think about how you would feel if you bumped into your best customer before you run out the door in the pair of sweats with the baggy butt and the hole in the knee. It's embarrassing to be dressed like a slob and have someone say, "Are you that guy on TV?" Trust me on that one.

2. Go easy on the perfume or cologne. I shouldn't smell you from across the room. Perfume is like Brylcreem: A little dab'll do ya.

3. Don't become a slave to trends. It's expensive and makes you look more like a person without any style than a person of style. If you want something that's trendy, don't spend much money on it, for it will soon be out of style.

4. Belly bags and fanny packs . . . don't. Really. Please. Just don't. In fact, if you travel outside the United States and want to make sure you look like a tourist, put on a fanny pack and athletic shoes.

5. When in doubt, wear black. Black is always appropriate. It makes you look richer, classier and, best of all, slimmer. (By the way, women have known this for years and never shared this helpful little bit of information. They never told us if we put it in black, it would look smaller. That's why I don't have any black underwear.)

6. It's okay to express your individuality. Holy crap, look at me! But there is a time when it's appropriate to tone it down. You can dress appropriately for the occasion and still express yourself.

7. It's okay to be different in your style. However, the more different you are, the better you have to be. Trust me, I know about this one. That's why I have to be really good!

When you are going out with your significant other, do him a favor before you go out, and try a little honesty. I am amazed when I see couples out and she looks great: heels, little black dress, jewelry, the works. And he looks like he just got back from a hiking trip. Ladies, say something. Don't go out with this bozo until he cleans it up.

Fashion Tips for Men

1. Ties should be tied so that the end of the tie, preferably the big end, hits at the bottom of the belt. If you are tall or longwaisted or have a fat gut, then buy extra-long ties so they will be long enough to reach your belt.

2. Ties should not advertise your favorite team or be covered with bottles of hot sauce, cartoon characters or dead rock musicians.

3. The above statement also applies to socks.

4. Shoes should always be shined. Loafers never go with a suit. Penny loafers don't really go with anything, Fonzie. And in my personal opinion, tassel loafers work only when you want everyone to consider you a pretentious goober named Biff.

5. Pants should hit your shoes. Not so long that you walk on them, but long enough to break (bend at the shoe). If I can see your socks while you are standing, then your pants are too short.

6. Be careful with knit shirts. If they are too tight, you will look fat. For the most part, if the knit stretches, the shirt is too tight. For all you bodybuilder guys who like to wear your shirts skintight: Don't. We get it—you work out—we're all proud for you. Now buy a shirt that fits.

7. Dress shirts do not come in short sleeves and short-sleeve shirts shouldn't be worn with a tie. Button-down shirts are not dress shirts; they are casual shirts and should not be worn with a suit. However, they may be worn with slacks and a sport coat.

Fashion Tips for Women

What do I know about women's fashion? Quite a lot. I read all the fashion magazines. I watch the Fashion Channel. I know all the designers and can spot a pair of Manolos across a crowded room. I am a man's man in every way, but I love women's fashion and I have opinions. Here they are:

1. Don't tie a coat or sweater around your waist. If you aren't a size two or smaller, then you are going to look like you have a huge butt. And don't think you are hiding your big butt by do-ing it—you are emphasizing it.

2. Don't wear white hose unless you work in a hospital and it's required dress for your nurse's uniform.

3. Just because it looks good on Heidi Klum doesn't mean it is going to look good on you. Everything looks good on Heidi Klum. The same probably doesn't apply to you. Wear clothes that fit your body type and emphasize your good features and play down your bad ones.

4. Salespeople lie. It is their job to say, "That looks darling on you!"

5. No Christmas sweaters. I know some of you love your Christmas sweaters—get over it. There are even Ugly Christmas Sweater parties where people wear these horrid creations. In fact, my family had its own party last year and to find the sweaters, I just went to eBay and typed in "ugly Christmas sweater," and hundreds of them showed up. That should be a clue as to what kind of fashion statement they make. If you aren't wearing it as a joke, you shouldn't be wearing it. The same rule applies to Halloween sweaters, Easter sweaters, Thanksgiving sweaters and any other holiday with something that can be woven into or embroidered onto a sweater.

6. Shoes make the outfit. Shoes can take a blah outfit and make it dazzling. Shoes can also take a dazzling outfit and make it blah. While high heels may be uncomfortable and even bad for you, remember men are pigs and we love them.

7. For the most part, hats make you look stupid. Though I suppose there are exceptions. If you are attending the Kentucky Derby, going to church on Easter or putting on a ball cap with a ponytail pulled through it, you can slide on this rule. Other than that, leave them to Queen Elizabeth. And doesn't *she* look nice?

8. VPL. Know what that means? Visible panty line. No one should be able to tell what kind of underwear you have on with your clothes covering it. That's information we just don't need. Dress accordingly.

Fashion Tips for Full-Figured People

1. Buy bigger clothes. If all of your lumps are visible, then your clothes are too tight. Tight clothes only make you look fatter than you really are, and trust me, you don't need the help.

2. For the big boys: Pull your pants up to the middle of your waist. If you wear your pants below your belly, you only look fatter. Your pants should hit you in the middle of your stomach. I love it when I hear some guy say he still wears a thirty-six-inch pant. His waist is easily forty-two inches but he wears his pants under his belly so he can say he is a thirty-six. Pull your pants up, pal! But don't pull them up until they are under your man boobs. Too high is just as bad as too low. Strive for the middle!

3. Don't decorate it. Bigger people should tone it down and not accentuate their size unless it is their intent to look like a circus tent. Plaids, flowers and gaudy prints are not your friends.

4. Larry's rule for fat people: The more skin you have, the less of it we need to see.

Oh, yeah, the answer is a resounding **no** to that old question, "Does this make my butt look fat?" Your butt *is* fat; the clothes are just proving it to the rest of the world.

Put on your big-boy pants.

I attended a charity event this year in Scottsdale, Arizona, where I live. It was a fairly pricey little function to attend, and I guess there were maybe five or six hundred people there. The suggested attire on the invitation said, "Sophisticated Chic—Dress to Impress." While it wasn't specific as to what that exactly meant, I understood, as I am sure most of you do. But I was amazed at the number of people who thought the rest of us were going to be impressed by their sophisticatedly chic T-shirts, shorts and Crocs sandals. Come on, people—be appropriate! What goes through the mind of any person who is getting ready to go to ANY event (other than a kegger on the beach) when you think you can wear a T-shirt and shorts, "Sophisticated Chic" aside?

I am sick of the lack of couth people show when they go out in the evening, especially when dining out in nice restaurants. I live in Scottsdale, Arizona, where it's hot—HELL hot most of the time—but that doesn't mean that it's okay to wear shorts 24/7. The same thing applies in Vegas—the Rat Pack would roll over in their graves if they witnessed the crappy way people dress when they go to the casinos. I'm not against being comfortable, by any means. But if we are going all out for comfort, why don't we all just wear muumuus?

I like shorts and I wear them a lot. I wear them to the beach and to play golf when it's more than 100 degrees and to a ball game or out during the daytime just about anyplace. Anyplace except where it isn't appropriate. And the one place where shorts are NEVER appropriate is when dining out after dark in a restaurant. (Yeah, I know, there are some restaurants where it is okay. Use your head—those aren't the restaurants I mean and you know it. Hooters is not where I'm talking about here!)

Here are some rules for when to wear your long pants:

If the place you are dining has cloth napkins,
you need to wear long pants.

If there are two forks on the table,
you need to wear long pants.

If your wife or date is wearing high heels,
you need to wear long pants.

If you are wearing black socks,
you need to wear long pants.

If they don't say, "You want fries with that?"
you need to wear long pants.

If it's dark outside,
you need to wear long pants.

If there is valet parking,
you need to wear long pants.

If they escort you to your table,
you need to wear long pants.

If your bill comes in a folder,
you need to wear long pants.

If no one else is wearing shorts,
you need to wear long pants.

If the invitation says, "Sophisticated Chic—Dress to Impress,"
you need to wear long pants.

Grow up, folks! You aren't a little kid any longer. . . . It's time to put on your big-boy pants and look like a grown-up.

WHAT HAVING BETTER FASHION SENSE WOULD DO FOR ME, AND WHY THAT'S IMPORTANT:

_____

_____

_____

_____

_____

_____

_____

_____

SOME THINGS I NEED TO CHANGE ABOUT THE WAY I DRESS:

_____

_____

_____

_____

_____

_____

_____

_____

_____

To Travel Better on Airplanes

You may think this is a ridiculous topic to include in a book like this. Then again, this book is about idiots, and if you ever want to see a bunch of idiots, go to the airport—there are many who work there. Also, as a guy who spends about 250 days a year on the road, I see a lot of people who are horrible at traveling. Take a few hints from a guy who knows about airline travel.

1. Regarding carry-on bags: Airlines have a little box to stick your bag in to make sure it will fit in the overhead compartment. If there is a question in your mind, then use the box. Get a clue about how big your bag is. Don't get on the plane with dozens of people behind you and then start trying to figure out how to make that big bag squish into that little bitty space.

2. When you walk down the aisle, put your carry-on bags in front of you so you don't bang people in the head. As a passenger sitting in an aisle seat, watch out for people who don't follow this rule. By the way, backpacks are for hikers and schoolchildren. Don't use them for traveling, and if you do, take them off your back before walking down the aisle.

3. Remember that the seat-back tray in front of you is attached to the back of someone else's seat. Don't pound on it, and don't let your child pound on it either. In fact, keep your kid as quiet as possible. It's a tight, uncomfortable space where noises are amplified, and your kid *is* bothering other people. I was recently on a plane where a couple had a little two-year-old who was going bonkers. They were making no effort to control their child. The little boy was banging on the seat-back tray and running up and down the aisle and screaming. While the parents seemed embarrassed and exasperated with the child's behavior, they weren't doing much about it either. A woman behind me turned to the couple and said, "Don't worry about it; we all love children and understand. It's okay." I turned and said, "Hey, Mary Poppins, not all of us understand. The kid is out of control and making the rest of us miserable." They all looked at me like I had horns growing out of my head. But after that, the parents did figure out a way to get their child under control so they wouldn't bother the mean man in front of them. Or the other 125 passengers.

4. Don't fart. Don't sneeze without your hand covering your honker. Don't cough without covering your mouth. Don't eat smelly things.

Not long ago, I was sitting on a plane and a very large woman sat down next to me and pulled out a big ziplock bag full of fried bacon and a two-pound bag of M&M's. No kidding. Imagine how good that smelled on the plane—and then imagine how good that was for her health.

Another woman behind me decided to change her baby's dirty diaper in her lap. How considerate of her not to take her sweet little baby's stinky butt into the restroom to clean it up.

While these are important things to remember regardless of where you are, it is especially important on airplanes because there is a limited amount of space and air; odors and germs travel faster and don't have anywhere to go.

5. Don't feel compelled to talk to your seatmate. In other words, it's okay to be polite and friendly and say hello, but then pay attention to whether your seatmate actually wants to talk. If she immediately buries her nose in a book or takes out a laptop to get some work done, chances are she's not interested. In my case, it is because I want to rest. I travel all the time and I want to use the flight time to rest and read. Be aware that there are people who don't want to talk to you. They don't care about your travel problems because they are dealing with their own. They don't want to know what you do for a living and don't want to tell you what the book they are reading is about. Some people just want to be left alone. Which means you shouldn't sigh loudly or moan and say things like "Oh, what a day!" to get your seatmate's attention.

6. Don't sit in the boarding area (or the bar) until they announce the final boarding call—only to rush to get on the plane before they shut the door and then open every overhead compartment, looking for a place to put your oversize bag. There is no place to put your bag. You got there too late. Don't complain, don't ask for help and don't mutter under your breath. It's your own fault—sit down and kick and push and smash that thing under the seat in front of you, and next time get on the plane when they call your boarding group number.

7. Don't travel with a pillow. People who carry their own personal pillows on trips are idiots. Like they don't have pillows where these people are going? I have traveled 250 days per year for nearly twenty years. I have stayed in hotels in cities all over the world, and so far, every single place I have traveled has had pillows. "But I can't sleep without my own pillow!" Grow up, you big baby, you aren't two years old! Leave your raggedy old pillow with the faded Strawberry Shortcake pillowcase on your bed and travel like a grown-up.

8. Shhh! That's right—be quiet. Just like odors carry, so does your voice. If you feel compelled to have a conversation with your neighbor, do it quietly. If you are wearing headphones, make sure I can't hear your music through your headphones. It's your music, not mine. Keep it to yourself. And cell phones? Holy crap, you don't have to scream at people; the technology is better than that.

I was recently on a plane that was in the boarding stages. I was all the way up in front, seated in the first-class section, yet I could clearly hear a woman on her cell phone in about row 30. If I could hear every word she was saying twenty-eight rows away, I know everyone else on the plane could, too. Whether she understood it or not, I am almost positive the person she was talking to on her cell phone could also hear her. In fact, the person could probably hear her without her cell phone! As a part of her conversation, she asked the person she was speaking with to call her back and then gave her cell phone number. I put her number into my own cell phone and dialed her up. When she answered, I told her I was sitting in first class and could hear every word of her conversation and I was sure everyone else on the plane could hear it as well. I asked her to speak more quietly when she received the call she was expecting because the rest of us found it distracting and rude and didn't have any interest in her conversation. She started screaming, "Who the hell are you? Where are you?" I stood up and waved at her with a big smile on my face. She hung up on me. None of us heard a peep out of her again.

9. When you ask someone to trade seats with you so you can sit by your friend or family member and they say no, accept it. Some people pay extra and plan a long time in advance to get the seat they want to sit in, so be accepting of their decision to keep their assigned seat. Besides, your seventeen-year-old daughter doesn't want to sit with you, regardless of what you think. She thinks you are boring and a pain in the butt to talk to: It's her job.

10. Mechanical problems are not the fault of the flight attendant. Bad weather is not the fault of the flight attendant. In fact, little that goes wrong with airline travel is ever the fault of the flight attendant. Which means, be nice to the flight attendants! It's not their fault. They can't get you there any faster. They aren't flying the plane or doing air traffic control or running the jet bridge. They aren't the ones making you late, so lay off.

11. Security and TSA. We all know it is tough. The other day, I followed a pilot through security and he had a bumper sticker on his flight bag that read, IF YOU AREN'T APPALLED, IT'S BECAUSE YOU HAVEN'T FLOWN LATELY. Stay calm. This one is tough for me because I have enough stories about the stupidity of the process to fill another entire book. But none of the horror stories we all have about TSA is going to change one thing. It's an idiotic process steeped in fear. It lacks logic. Save yourself the grief and strip it off. Do it as quickly as you can. Don't talk about it or even spend much time thinking about it. Get through it as best you can without having your head explode. My only real suggestion is to get there plenty early so you won't add to the stress caused by the stupidity of the process.

Flying causes enough anxiety without adding to your own or someone else's. Take a chill pill, folks; you'll get there.

WHY I WOULD BENEFIT FROM BEING A BETTER TRAVELER:

_____

_____

_____

_____

_____

_____

_____

To Make a Better World

1. Love more—hate less.

2. Recycle.

3. Be involved. Don't just be a spectator.

4. Support organizations that feed and clothe those who need it.

5. Take care of the Earth.

6. Don't litter.

7. Make at least one other person smile every day.

8. Buy things from little kids.

9. Don't talk in movie theaters.

10. Never smack your gum.

**WHY MAKING A BETTER WORLD IS
IMPORTANT TO ME:**

_____
_____
_____
_____
_____
_____
_____
_____
_____

THE SHORT LISTS

To get started:
Just start. Don't complicate it more than that.

To quit smoking:
Stop putting cigarettes in your mouth.

To deal with criticism:
Don't. Rise above needing the approval of others.

To have a positive attitude:
Don't bother. A positive attitude won't make you
more successful anyway!

To avoid problems:
You can't. Problems are a part of life. The only people
without problems are dead.

To get others to change:
You can't. People change when they want to, not when you
want them to.

To win every argument:
You can't. Sometimes you lose. It happens. Deal with it.
Besides, about half the arguments you get into, you deserve
to lose. Why? Because you are wrong. There are other
arguments you get into that you never should have gotten
into to begin with, and it doesn't matter if you win or not.
Win the ones that count.

To age gracefully:
Why would you want to do that? Go out kicking and
screaming. Old age is not for sissies. Stay fit, stay fun and
kick ass 'til you die.

FOR ALL OF YOU WHO ARE NOW SAYING, "BUT I WANTED TO KNOW HOW TO . . ."

I can't tell you how to get along better with your loser
brother-in-law, or what to do when your daughter calls you because her fiancé called the wedding off, or what to feed your
dog when it has a temperature. Yes, I really get those kinds of

questions. And yes, some people will criticize the book because I didn't cover enough specific circumstances and I didn't address their own particular personal dilemma. To all those who are now thinking that way—and trust me, there are plenty of them—let me just say, "Holy crap, people! Grow the hell up. Use your friggin' heads! Some of this crap you have to figure out on your own!"

IDIOTS:
THE FINAL
CHAPTERS

CHAPTER SIX

IT'S EASY TO KEEP BEING AN IDIOT!

"What is easy to do is also easy not to do."

Jim Rohn

Many years ago when I first became a student of self-improvement, I discovered that quote by Jim Rohn. Those eleven little words made a major impact on my thinking at the time. They still do. Whenever I think about how easy it would be to get off my own fatter-than-it-ought-to-be ass and go for a walk or do some other exercise, I am reminded that it is just as easy not to do it. Whenever I think about how easy it would be to go write a blog or a chapter for an upcoming book, I remember that it would be just as easy not to do it. When I think how easy it would be to call a buddy to catch up, I know it would be just as easy not to do it.

It's easy to become successful. It's easy to lose weight. It's easy to have better relationships. It's easy to do better at work. It's easy to have more money. All of it is easy. It is just as easy not to do these things, too.

It's not hard.

Please don't buy into the idea that success is hard to achieve. Those who tell you that success is hard are undermining your success and playing to your weaker side. They are treating you like a sucker. Don't be a sucker for them. Shun the idea that success is hard. It isn't. The people who believe success is hard want it to be hard. They want success to be hard so they will have an excuse for not being successful. It's their primary excuse. If you have been living as one of those people who believe success is hard, then that's why you haven't been successful so far.

I have proven to you how easy success is. Every one of the lists I have given you is filled with things that are easy to do. You can't argue with that. There isn't one thing on any one of my lists that is hard. As I warned in the introduction, my information has a high Duh Factor.

And as Shakespeare pointed out so eloquently, "There's the rub." The problem is that success is almost too simple. If it were harder, people would appreciate it more and work harder to achieve it. The fact that it isn't hard makes people lack respect for it and those who have achieved it. For them it seems easier to ridicule success than to achieve success.

In *The Adventures of Tom Sawyer*, Mark Twain wrote about Tom:

> *He had discovered a great law of human action, without knowing it—namely, that in order to make a man or a boy covet a thing, it is only necessary to make the thing difficult to obtain.*

That is a huge factor in why people aren't successful. Success isn't difficult enough to obtain. If it were harder to obtain, people would covet it more. While it seems like it is difficult to obtain, that is a lie perpetuated by the unsuccessful.

So what is the solution?

The three words that say it all: because you can.

Because you can.

Those three words are the answer to all of the reasons you should be—no, you have to be—successful.

Why be rich? Because you can.

Why have great relationships? Because you can.

Why be healthy and live a long time? Because you can.

Why be smart? Because you can.

Why be successful in every single area of your life? Because you can.

You are obligated to become as much as you can be simply because you can!

It is never that you *can't* do better. It is always that you *won't* do better. Which means success goes back to something I have referred to throughout the book: your decision. It is your decision whether you will or whether you won't succeed. Choose "will."

Say these words aloud right now:

I will be successful because I can be successful. I know success comes from recognizing my mistakes and taking responsibility for them. I know that success comes from educating myself so I will be smarter. I know that success comes from taking action on what I know and being willing to do whatever it takes to make my goals become my reality. I take action on these ideas because I owe it to myself and to my family. I do all of this because I can!

DON'T LIKE MY AFFIRMATION? NO PROBLEM. WRITE YOUR OWN RIGHT NOW.

CHAPTER SEVEN

WHAT DO YOU THINK?

It is time to judge the book. You finished it. You have an opinion. What is it?

Why do I ask? Believe me, it's not because I want you to write me and tell me. I appreciate it when people enjoy my work, but I am not asking for personal feedback here, so no e-mails or letters of praise are required. I am certainly not asking so you can write to tell me what a waste of time it has been or how you disagree with me about this point or that idea. If you hated it or thought it was a waste of time, find someone to complain to who gives a crap, because I don't. I have given you my thoughts, opinions and ideas between the covers of this book. It's done. It's too late to do anything about it. It's in print forever and I can't and wouldn't change a word of it, even if that were possible. I am asking you to judge the book, not me. Besides, your opinion of this book isn't for me—it's for you.

I told you that my purpose in writing this book was to get your attention. It was to make some bold statements to get you to look at your life and consider the idea that you might be sabotaging your success. I want you to ask yourself whether I accomplished my purpose.

Every bit of input you get from every source moves you in one direction or the other. Nothing is neutral. You have to start thinking about the impact of the "input" you are allowing into your life. Is the input you are accepting into your life moving you closer to your goals or farther away from your goals?

Every conversation you are involved in moves you closer to your goals or farther away from your goals. Every television program you watch does the same thing. So does every phone call. And every friend. Probably the biggest input you ever allow into your life is the content of a book you read. Books have such a strong impact because it takes time to read a book. Unlike a television show that is over in an hour or a conversation that lasts a few minutes, a book takes some real time to get through. You reach a level of intimacy with a book that allows you to read it, put it down, ponder what has been presented and make decisions based on the information you have read.

Since everything either moves you closer to your goals or farther away, which direction did this book move you? Are you now closer to your goals or farther away? Do you have a clearer picture of what you need to do to achieve what you want? Do you have some tools you didn't have before?

How I evaluate a book

When I reach the end of any book, either fiction or nonfiction, I normally close it and then do a fast ten-second assessment of the book.

The highest accolade from me when I close a book is when I say something along the lines of, "That was good. I know my buddy Mark would love this." When you immediately know someone else who would love the book you just finished, it means you want to share your experience with him. You respect the book enough to share it with someone you respect. At that point, if it is a fiction book, I give it to that person. If it is a nonfiction book, I buy them their own copy because I mark up my nonfiction books and make notes so I can refer to them later. I have read books that were so good, I ordered a dozen copies for my buddies so they could enjoy my discovery as much as I did.

If I finish a book and say to myself, "Not bad," and then stick it on a shelf, I know that book will end up in a box that will be sent to the next charity book drive.

Sometimes what comes to mind is, "Holy crap! I've got to go to work! There is so much good stuff in here that I have to get started right now!" That is a great feeling for sure because few books are actually that good. Admittedly, I sometimes get overwhelmed and end up doing very little with the information I've read because there is simply too much to do. While I like books that teach me a lot of stuff, I don't always get through all the stuff because there is too much of it.

Then there is the book that has one nugget. When I close the book, I say, "There is my one thing." I am always looking for my "one thing." Conversations, lectures, sermons and books . . . they all have one thing. One overriding lesson to teach—or at least they should.

I have discovered my one thing in books that had only one thing. The rest of the book was worthless drivel. However, that one thing still made the book worthwhile. I had to read 250 pages to find that one amazing sentence that helped me earn more money or taught me how to live a better life. Two hundred and fifty pages to find one sentence. Was it a waste? No, because I got my sentence! One sentence can change your life.

Some authors have expectations that are too high. They try to teach too much. They give you so much stuff you could do that you end up doing nothing at all. Please don't let that be the case with this book. I have given you a lot of stuff, but I don't expect you to do it all. Not at first. You can always come back to the book and start on something else later.

My goal for you in this book is that you will walk away with one good lesson from it. One big thing that enables you to close the book and say, "This is it! I need to do this today."

If I have given you a nugget that can move you closer to your goal, this book is a winner for you.

Do you have a nugget? Write it down. Commit thought to paper.

MY ONE THING:

_____

_____

_____

_____

_____

_____

_____

_____

_____

_____

Now you are ready to close the book and get started.

ACKNOWLEDGMENTS

Thanks to my wife, Rose Mary. Every time I'm an idiot, she lovingly reminds me I can do better.

To Tyler and Patrick, my boys and best friends.

To Vic Osteen, my manager and friend, who protects me from the idiots as best he can.

To my editor, Jessica Sindler. Trust me when I say how hard we both worked on this book!

To my publisher, Bill Shinker, who through a few books, a few great dinners, a few glasses of wine and some great conversation has become a good friend.

To Jay Mandel, my agent, who guides me, advises me and reminds me to keep typing.

To my buddies in the American Speakers Society (A.S.S.). These guys put up with me and I put up with them out of respect, friendship and mutual idiocy. That's all I can say about this matter, because the Number One Rule of A.S.S. is "We don't talk about A.S.S."

To Ralphie, my English bulldog. He calms me down, slows my heart rate, makes me smile and loves me when no one else would even consider it.

To Butter, my French bulldog: the princess and the bitch. I like her kisses.